CHURCH *of* COWARDS

CHURCH of COWARDS

A Wake-Up Call to Complacent Christians

MATT WALSH

Regnery Publishing
WASHINGTON, D.C.

Regnery® is a registered trademark and its colophon is a trademark of Salem Communications Holding Corporation

ISBN: 978-1-68451-366-6
LCCN: 2019955269

First trade paperback edition published 2022

Published in the United States by
Regnery Publishing
A Division of Salem Media Group
Washington, D.C.
www.Regnery.com

Manufactured in the United States of America

10 9 8 7 6 5 4 3 2 1

Books are available in quantity for promotional or premium use. For information on discounts and terms, please visit our website: www.Regnery.com

Contents

CHAPTER ONE

Christians Not Worth Killing

*They followed worthless idols and became
worthless themselves.*

—*Jeremiah 2:5*[1]

Tthere are still some Christians in this country who worry that
heathen hordes may one day arrive on our shores, armed
with guns and knives and bombs, to crush our Christian way
of life and destroy the American church. They worry that Christendom will come under brutal assault by these hypothetical savages—
that they, clinging tearfully to their Bibles, will be dragged into the
town square and beheaded in front of cheering, bloodthirsty throngs.
They worry that we believers in the West may finally suffer the same
persecution those in the East have faced for two thousand years.

They flatter themselves.

Let us imagine that this heathen horde does show up one day,
swords in hand, revved and ready to butcher some Christians. Consider their confusion upon landing here. Looking about, they expect
to see ample evidence of Christianity in this Christian nation, but
instead they have stumbled upon a very strange sort of paganism.

They do not find any clear indication that the people of this Christian land worship the Christian God. They see instead the worship of actors, of politicians, of athletes, of imaginary figures on television. They discover, too, the worship of things, of objects like electronic gadgets and cars and houses. Most of all, it would seem, the people of this Christian land worship the great and magnificent god called the Self.

This is all very confusing for our heathens. They had pictured an America filled with pious, modest, prayerful believers, but instead they find silly, shallow, oversexed, nihilistic zombies who live vicariously through their phones, which they have stocked with photographs of their own faces. They find that modesty is mocked, discipline is scorned, and obedience is rejected on principle. They find materialism, hedonism, secularism, avowed atheism, and unavowed atheism. The only thing they have trouble locating is Christianity.

As our heathens begin to conduct a closer investigation, they discover that the nuclear family is in disarray here in this Christian country. Fewer than half of our children live with both biological parents in the home. Divorce is commonplace and unquestioned. Sometimes the dissolution of a marriage is celebrated with a divorce party. How odd this is for a Christian country, the heathens note, considering that the Christian Lord and Savior expressly forbade divorce.

They notice that all manner of sexual perversion is accepted and legitimized. Homosexuals, far from being called to purity, are encouraged to "marry" each other. Raucous parades are held across the country to applaud sodomy. Perversion is promoted and advertised everywhere. The heathens see that some of the men here in this Christian country dress in skirts and pretend to be women, and everyone else plays along with the charade. They see drag queen story hours at libraries, cross-dressing child models on television, and many other forms of debauchery—all tolerated and even celebrated.

They discover that pornography is a multibillion-dollar industry. Children here in this Christian country start watching porn when they're thirteen years old.[2] And many of those same children have already been robbed of their innocence at school, where they are taught about masturbation and anal sex and their nurses hand out contraceptives.[3]

As the heathens wander around confused, bewildered, they see a nondescript office building with the words "Planned Parenthood" written on the side. They walk through the door and down the hall and find a man in a lab coat extracting a child from a woman's birth canal one piece at a time. They soon learn that such a procedure is carried out hundreds of times a day in this Christian country. Over sixty million human babies have been dismembered and discarded,[4] legally, and with the enthusiastic approval or apathetic acceptance of a majority of the population. "Even we don't kill babies," the heathens say to each other in disgust.

They are perplexed. There are supposed to be 240 million Christians within America's borders.[5] Where did they go? Did they float into space? Did they fall into the ocean and drown? It is like the mysterious disappearance of the settlers at Roanoke, except in this case it is the church that has disappeared—and not from just one island, but from the entire continent.

The would-be persecutors stop a pedestrian and inquire as to the whereabouts of these elusive Christian creatures. He points them down the road to something he describes as a "church." *Yes*, the heathens think, *finally! We shall descend upon them and crush them!*

But they are profoundly confused as they approach the alleged house of worship. From the outside it looks like a post office or a medical clinic. There is not a cross or religious symbol in sight. The name on the sign says something like "New Horizons" or "Cross Point." It seems less like a house of worship and more like a rehab center for wealthy drug abusers.

The would-be oppressors wander inside and find a bunch of people sitting around in casual clothing, sipping Starbucks, listening to a mediocre rock band perform a pop song. Nobody is demonstrating anything approaching reverence. There is no sign that anything sacred is happening here, or that anyone believes it is. Then out onto the stage strides a hip young man with perfect hair wearing skinny jeans and a deep V-neck. He launches into a series of self-help maxims and inspirational platitudes. The man—a "pastor," he claims—speaks about God in vague and general terms. But not the Christian God. The God this man is telling his audience about seems to be a magical genie whose only function is to satisfy their appetites. There is no judgment in this God. He is a Divinity who sits back passively, waiting for His children to arrive into a Paradise that they are all absolutely certain to enter, no matter how they live.

The heathens standing in the back, now with venti lattes in hand, look with shock at one another. This is not Christianity. At least it is not a Christianity worth persecuting. They leave disappointed.

After wandering around the neighborhood for a while, they come across another supposed church. This one has the appearance of a basketball stadium or a shopping mall—or maybe a sci-fi villain's futuristic compound—and it is packed to the rafters with thousands of noisy spectators. The heathens walk through the doors, right by the coffee stand, past the gift shop, through the food court, and into a giant auditorium with a humongous stage adorned not with crosses, but with a globe, or possibly a picture of a tree. They see video cameras everywhere. They see fancy lighting and expensive audiovisual equipment. People in brightly colored T-shirts are handing out brochures. Another rock band is playing.

A smiley, pleasant-looking man walks on stage in a fancy suit. He has a friendly countenance and an engaging speaking style, but his message is hollow and deceptively cynical. He tells his audience that if they believe in God they will be blessed with wealth and good health. He preaches a kind of mercenary faith, where the believer believes only so far as it benefits his temporal life. The sermon sounds like one long refutation of the Beatitudes. This "pastor," like the first one, says nothing about sin, redemption, repentance, holiness, or obedience. He is like a less religious Oprah.

The heathens are getting frustrated. If this is Christianity, it's far too weak, self-centered, and effeminate to make killing its adherents worth it.

Further down the road they happen across yet another church. Their enthusiasm for their mission revives as—they are interested to see—this one actually looks like a Christian church. But there is a rainbow flag hanging on the side of it, and through a stained glass window they can see a middle-aged woman sporting a crew cut and priestly garb. Besides the priestess, the building is virtually empty. They don't bother going inside.

Finally they come to a bland, ugly, office-like building that at least has a Christian name, like St. Mark's or Holy Family. They walk through the lobby and into something that obscurely resembles a sanctuary. They see a smattering of old, bored people wearing T-shirts and sitting on cushioned pews chatting softly with each other. A choir of baby boomers in jeans, standing in the place of honor at the front of the church, begins playing something that sounds like a cross between elevator music and a campfire song. "Let us build a house where love can dwell . . . Built of hopes and dreams and visions,"[6] the choir sings. The heathens feel conflicting urges—to laugh, and to vomit.

Out proceeds a priest, flanked by altar girls and singing the terrible ditty as he strolls nonchalantly down the aisle. After a few prayers are said—or, rather, sung badly—the priest rises to deliver his homily. It is lengthy and rambling and utterly pointless. He offers no moral guidance whatsoever. He doesn't acknowledge the cultural horrors that these heathens have themselves witnessed. It appears to the heathens that this priest is actually *trying* to be irrelevant. He succeeds. On and on he blathers about something or other—friendship or tolerance or kindness. In both tone and substance, he sounds like an HR rep giving a seminar on teamwork. Shortly after he finishes speaking, a mass of people swarm the altar, grab plates full of communion hosts from the priest, and begin passing them out to the other members of the church. The scene looks like a Chipotle during the lunch rush. The heathens could swear they heard someone ask for a side of guacamole.

They turn around quietly and leave. Nothing they have seen here is worth destroying. Besides, they need to get outside before the choir starts singing again.

The dejected gang of would-be oppressors convenes in the parking lot and they discuss their next step. Most of them want to head back East, where there are plenty of real Christians to murder. Others disagree. Finally, the matter is decided. They will make one last attempt to smoke out a few real Christians in America before they officially give up and go home. So they run back to the church with Skinny-Jeans Pastor, and the church with Smiley Pastor, and the church with Lesbian Priest, and the church with Teamwork Priest, and with blades drawn they kidnap all of the ministers and about twenty congregants from each place. They collect a total of a hundred "Christians," drag them out into the street, and line them up. The Head Heathen steps forward.

"All right. We were looking to martyr some Christians today, but it looks like we're going to have to settle for you lot. So we demand that you abandon your Christian God and worship our gods. Renounce your faith now, or die where you stand!"

The crowd stirs. The captives look terrified, but also a bit confused.

One of them speaks up. "Well, I would never suggest that our God is the only legitimate one," he says. "All faiths are equal."

"Yes," another agrees. "We're tolerant of all viewpoints. We'll gladly worship your gods as well as ours. Inclusivity is our motto! Here, have a brochure!"

"All gods are the same," Lesbian Priest explains. "We have our conception of the divine, and you have yours. Nobody's belief is wrong or right. Nobody can lay claim to absolute truth."

She appears to be expressing the general consensus.

Head Heathen tries again. "Okay, let me narrow it down. You must renounce your belief that the man you call Jesus Christ is God."

But this doesn't help. A large number of American Christians, ignorant of the fundamentals of their own theology, actually believe that Jesus is a created being.[7]

"Well, actually, God made Jesus. Jesus is God's son, or something, is the idea, I think," someone in the group stammers.

"Yeah, I mean he's not *God* God, right?" chimes in another.

"It doesn't matter. Let's not get bogged down in pointless doctrine!"

"Right! This isn't the Middle Ages, after all."

Head Heathen is exasperated. He is now searching desperately for a reason to kill at least a few of these people. "Fine. Fine. Then just generally renounce your religion or—,"

"Religion?" Skinny-Jeans Pastor pipes up. "Oh, we don't have a religion. Religion is outdated and suppressive."

"Exactly! We have a relationship with Jesus, not a religion!"

"Relationships, not religion," a dozen people shout in unison.

"Right. Okay." Head Heathen is running out of patience. "Then just say that you renounce everything in the Bible, and we'll leave it at that."

"No problem," says one of the assembled. "There are many out-moded and frankly archaic things in the Bible. All of the stuff about Hell, for instance, can't be taken literally."

This comment is met with resounding approval.

"I saw something on YouTube about how Moses didn't even exist," someone else offers.

Smiley Pastor chimes in. "As long as you love Jesus in your heart, it's not so much necessary to follow all of the strict and narrow-minded rules in a book that was written thousands of years ago!"

"Yes, just think of how Paul talks about women! Surely we've grown past all that!"

"Someone told me once that the Bible says that only those who do the will of God will enter Heaven. If that's in there, it would be quite dangerous to take it literally."

"Yes, all of that stuff about taking up our cross and so forth. We can certainly take or leave all of that. Just as long as we believe in God."

"But even if we don't, that's OK too."

"Yes, of course."

"Of course."

"We can't judge."

"No, we mustn't ever judge."

"No judgment!"

Head Heathen now turns to Teamwork Priest. "Okay, priest. Surely you must disagree with these other people. Your church is very specific about its doctrines. Now publicly disavow those teachings or lose your head right here and now!"

"Many of us are very hopeful that the church will soon come out of the Dark Ages," the priest answers. "I certainly won't die for its rules—there are so many that need to be updated. Ask me to martyr myself for my church's outdated teaching on marriage, for example, and I simply could not do it in good conscience."

"Love wins!" someone from his church declares.

"We're not haters."

"Yes, and we must get rid of the anti-divorce propaganda."

"Far too rigid."

"Yes, too rigid!"

"So rigid!"

"Rigid!"

"And the church still says it's a sin to use contraception!"

"They still say that? Wow. What century is this?"

Head Heathen looks down in despair. He has given up hope.

Just then, one person, one in the hundred, steps out from the crowd.

"I believe," he announces in a resolute voice. "I believe in God, the Father Almighty, Creator of Heaven and earth; and in Jesus Christ, His only Son, our Lord; Who was conceived by the Holy Spirit, born of the Virgin Mary, suffered under Pontius Pilate, was crucified, died, and was buried. He descended into Hell; the third day He arose again from the dead. He ascended into Heaven, and sits at the right hand of God, the Father Almighty; from thence He shall come to judge the living and the dead. I believe in the Holy Spirit, the Holy Catholic Church, the communion of Saints, the forgiveness of sins, the resurrection of the body, and life everlasting."

The others look towards him in horror. He continues.

"I believe in the authority of scripture. I believe in all of the teachings that Christianity has professed for two thousand years. I believe in Heaven and Hell, in the necessity of repentance and obedience, in the saving work of Christ on the cross. I believe I must carry my cross as Christ carried His. I believe that not all religions are equal. I believe that only Christianity is true. I believe that those who do not repent and follow Christ are in danger of damnation. I believe that only through Christ does anyone enter eternal life. I believe in the indissoluble nature of marriage, in the dignity of human life, in the sanctity of the family. I believe that we are called to be chaste, modest, and humble. I believe that the Christian life is something distinct and visible and that if I am not living it in a distinct and visible way then I am not living it at all. I believe, do you hear me? I believe!"

Head Heathen is relieved, ecstatic. He has finally found one. A real one. He takes his sword and puts it to the Christian's throat. He can hear the man praying the Our Father quietly. The Christian takes one last breath and prepares to go home. But just then, Lesbian Priest raises her voice. "This man is not one of us. He's no Christian! He's a fundamentalist whack job. He doesn't speak for the rest of us!"

"He's a bigot!"

"Yeah, so intolerant!"

"And close-minded!"

"Homophobic!"

"Transphobic!"

"Xenophobic!"

"Crucify him!"

The crowd is in a frenzy, all shouting and cursing the Christian. The pastors and priests are leading the charge. Head Heathen steps back. "There is no reason to kill this man," he says to his friends. "He is but one voice in a hundred, drowned out by the other ninety-nine."

Sorrowfully, gloomily, they walk back to their boats and sail away. They were not able to crush our Christian way of life—because we don't have a Christian way of life. They were not able to destroy the church because there wasn't much of a church left in America to destroy. They were not able to behead the Christians because they couldn't find Christians to behead. They unsheathed their swords only to discover that what they came to kill was already dead. They had traveled all that way to persecute a corpse.

CHAPTER TWO

The Broad Road That Leads to Destruction

Enter through the narrow gate. For wide is the gate and broad is the road that leads to destruction, and many enter through it.

—Matthew 7:13

G od promised Abraham that He would not destroy Sodom if He found ten righteous people there. He did not find them. Sodom was destroyed. I sometimes wonder if He would be able to find His ten here in America, the new Sodom.

It is clear that we are no longer living in a Christian country. Christianity is dying here, and dying rapidly. The Christian faith can never pass away from the world, but it can be rejected by men and by nations. A man cannot remove Christ from the universe, but he can remove himself from Christ. A nation cannot chase the church from the face of the earth, but it can chase the church from its borders.

Today, around 70 percent of Americans claim to be Christian.[1] This number represents a marked decline, but the problem is not the decline in professed believers. If we had simply lost 10 or 20 percent, but still we had 70 percent who were really and truly on fire with the faith, there would be far less cause for concern. But the problem with the 70 percent is that it is not really 70 percent. The 70 percent is mostly composed of the sort of Christians who cannot be readily distinguished from atheists.

Indeed, the average American believer shares many similarities with the average American unbeliever. If you were to follow him around, track his movements, listen to his conversations, observe how he spends his free time (much like our iPhones already do), you would find no hard evidence that he believes anything at all lies beyond the veil of physical existence. He speaks just like the non-Christians, dresses just like them, carries himself as they do, watches all of the same television shows, consumes the same kind of media, indulges in the same vices, and feels the same lack of guilt for those indulgences. Everything is the same.

A Fog of Self-Deception

Ask the average American Christian to tell you how his life would be different if he didn't believe in Christ, and he will struggle to provide a single example. And this fact will not trouble him. He is supremely confident in his own spiritual complacency. He laughs at the very notion that God might send him to Hell. He has no problem believing that some people are damned—a lot of people, even—but not him. He lives in a fog of cowardly and comfortable delusion, and it grows thicker by the day.

The fog consists of a whole tangled mass of self-deceptions, some that we say out loud and some that we think to ourselves but would never say. It is those self-deceptions, those comforting delusions propelling us along the broad road that leads to destruction, that I hope to unravel in this book.

These self-deceptions, ironically, do not originate with the self. If we take our faith seriously, we will recognize them as Satan's handiwork. They are part of the extraordinarily effective battle plan that the Evil One has devised for the West. It is quite a different plan from the one he has been using in other parts of the world. Indeed, it would seem that he has only two strategies, and they lie on opposite ends of the spectrum. The first tactic is the simplest and most direct: kill the Christians. We see this unfolding across the world on an unprecedented scale. We hear about it on the news only sparingly, and never with the word "persecution" attached. But still the ground all over the globe is soaked in the blood of Christian martyrs.

Of course, the extermination of Christians in the East is ignored by American Christians and the church in this country just as completely as it is ignored by the media. We don't care. Not really. It is all too far away for us to notice. Too distant both in geography and experience. We carry on, then, as if the church is not under siege, as if war is not being waged upon us all.

The situation brings to mind the scene surrounding the Battle of Bull Run at the start of the Civil War. The Union so expected to win, and to win so easily, that Union sympathizers came out to the battlefield with blankets and picnic baskets. They sat off on the sidelines, lounging in the shade and drinking tea while an awful battle was fought in the distance. The picnickers would soon be grabbing their blankets and their baskets and running for their lives—the fight did not play out as they had anticipated—but the silliness, arrogance, and obliviousness of those spectators reminds me of the church in the West. We are relaxing, having our picnic, and eating our sandwiches, even as a violent and desperate fight rages on. Men are bleeding and dying and crying out in anguish while we nap comfortably in the shade. I would say that we are like the apostles in Gethsemane, but that would be giving us too much credit. Their spirit was willing while their flesh was weak. Our spirit is weak and our flesh even weaker.

A recent report tells us that Christian persecution is worse now than it has ever been in history.[2] Christians in Afghanistan, Somalia, Sudan, Pakistan, North Korea, Libya, Iraq, Yemen, Iran, Egypt, and many other countries are regularly imprisoned, tortured, beaten, raped, and martyred. Their churches are destroyed. Their houses burned. They meet and worship in secret, risking their lives in the process. They live every moment in constant danger.

There are many examples of this persecution that I could mention here, but I'd like to point to just one example from a couple of years ago, because I find it especially tragic and instructive, and I think it provides a striking contrast between the Middle Eastern brand of Christian and the Western brand.

A group of Egyptian Christians were in buses headed to a monastery in the desert. Islamist militants boarded the vehicles with guns, but they did not begin shooting right away. Instead, they pulled the passengers out and interrogated them. The pilgrims were first asked if they were Christian and then told to abandon Christ and convert to Islam. When each person refused to renounce his faith, he was shot in the head or the throat. Apparently all of the victims, even the children, died heroically in this way.[3] They would rather die than let go of Christ. And so they did die, and now they are forever in Our Lord's embrace. They let go of the world and fell straight into the arms of God.

Now, imagine confronting this yourself. Imagine what would be happening in your mind as you kneel there in the sand with the cold barrel of a gun pressing against your temple. There are two questions, remember. You must choose martyrdom twice.

First: "Are you Christian?"

You can escape death right here. All you need to say is "No." One word. One syllable. One syllable will save your life. That's all it will take. Just tell them no. You don't even have to believe it in your heart.

It's just a word. *No. No.* Say it, you scream to yourself. Say it. *No. No.* But the Holy Spirit comes over you and steadies your soul. You reach into a reservoir of courage you didn't know you had available, and you speak the simple truth. "Yes."

Second: "Will you renounce Christ and convert to Islam?"

Perhaps you didn't know there would be a second question. You thought they'd kill you after you answered affirmatively to the first. But now you have another chance to save yourself. Another chance to avoid a violent death out here in the middle of nowhere. The Devil whispers to you, "This is a message from God. He wants you to live. You have things to do. You have a family. You have a purpose on earth. Just say yes. Yes. Say yes and renounce. Say yes and betray Christ. He will understand. He does not expect you to be unreasonable." Most people would say yes, wouldn't they? It's a perfectly normal response. You mustn't be extreme, after all. But again, the Holy Spirit gives you strength, and you see Christ on the cross looking gently down at you: *Stand firm,* Christ says in your heart, *and today you will be with me in paradise.* So you take a breath, the last you will ever take on earth, you look your persecutor in the eyes, and with great calm and something almost like joy you say, "No."

How many of us have a faith like that? The Egyptian martyrs were willing to give up everything for Christ. How many of us are willing to give up anything—let alone everything? Most of us will lash out bitterly if we are asked to make any sacrifice at all, any adjustment to our lives, any change to our lifestyles. We will shriek in horror if anyone suggests, say, that we give up watching certain television shows or listening to certain music. We will explode in fury if anyone questions whether a Christian ought to watch pornography, or dress provocatively, or use profanity. We will laugh and mock and practically spit at any critic who dares to look at something we do, something we enjoy, something that gives us pleasure, and question whether it is proper. Most of us, if we are being perfectly honest, cannot think of one thing—one measly thing—that we greatly enjoy and have the means to do yet have stopped doing because we know it is inconsistent with our faith. I do not believe that I exaggerate when I say that the average American Christian has never given up one single thing for Christ.

I survey my own life as I write these words, and I see myself in a constant state of flight. Fleeing from sacrifice. Fleeing from suffering. I have rarely felt any pain or undergone any trial without kicking and screaming and trying to wriggle myself out of it. Our culture actively fosters this kind of cowardice. And now many of us have descended into a state of total worldliness. We have compared God's program to the world's program and opted for the latter, because it does not involve suffering.

So, give up our lives? Not a chance on earth. Put a gun to our head and we will do whatever you ask. There really is no need for the gun to our head. You could just put it to our televisions.

Christ has already told us what it means to follow Him. *Give up everything*, He commands. *Embrace your suffering. Carry your cross. Go hungry for Me. Bleed for Me. Die for Me.* "For whoever wants to save their life will lose it, but whoever loses their life for me will find it" (Matthew 16:25). Christians all across the Middle East, North Africa, and Asia have found their lives because they heard these words of Christ and took them literally.

Just think of what these martyrs were doing in the first place when they were killed. They were traveling out into the desert on a pilgrimage to pray at a monastery, despite the enormous risk that such a journey entails in a Muslim country. And what about us? Many of us can't be bothered to get up on a Sunday morning and drive twelve minutes to church. Our churches aren't in the desert. There aren't any Islamic militants patrolling the area, looking to put a bullet in our skulls and turn our children into slaves. What's our excuse? We don't want to get up. It's a hassle. It's boring. The seats aren't comfortable. We had an argument with someone at church and it might be awkward to see them. We don't like the sermons. The pastor was rude to us once. We don't "feel welcome." And so on.

Why Aren't You Shouting?

Sure, we've come up with theological excuses for not going to church, not changing our lifestyles, not really doing anything at all. We've found a verse or two that justify our laziness in our minds. This is the one area of religion where we exert some effort: in finding excuses to not be religious.

But our brothers and sisters in the East know nothing of these excuses. They can't conceive of why we'd even want to find them. They look at us and say with exasperation: *You can be as Christian as you want and nobody will hurt you. Nobody will kill you. You can shout about Christ from the rooftops. So why aren't you on the rooftops? Why aren't you shouting?*

Well, we might lose Facebook friends. Someone might accuse us of being weird. And, besides, if we start being really Christian then we might feel guilty about all of the gossiping we do at work, all the lies we tell, all the sexual sins we commit, all the porn we watch on our computers while our wives and children are asleep. We might feel ashamed of the fact that we drink too much and spend too much of our money on frivolous things, and that we give nothing to charity, and that we make no sacrifices at all, and that we live just like everyone else lives. That's what's stopping us.

In other words, nothing is stopping us. We're stopping ourselves. We are comfortable—and consumed by our comforts.

This is Satan's strategy for us. This is how the church has been subjugated in America. No shot has been fired, yet we Christians in the West have bowed in submission. We have been brought to our knees by an enemy wielding a feather pillow stuffed with a collection of comfortable lies. The Christians overseas get the stick. We get the carrot. And we will do anything for the carrot. We will fall to our faces and worship the carrot like a god.

Kill us? Why? We are no threat to Satan's master plan. A Christian in Afghanistan is a threat. He must be destroyed. It's the only way. But a lazy, soft, equivocating Christian in the West? There is no need to persecute him. He is not worthy of it. Just give him a television and the internet and let him drift into oblivion. Satan's instructions to his minions are clear: If a man is walking into Hell of his own accord, don't interfere. Walk ahead of him instead, and make sure the coast is clear. Whisper encouragement in his ear. Support him in his self-deception.

Satan's legions in America have figured out the secret: Don't put a gun to their heads and tell them to stop being Christian. Don't appeal to their fear, because if you do that you may accidentally awaken their courage. And then your plan is in trouble. If your persecution produces a bunch of passionate, courageous Christians, then you'll have to kill every last one of them. If you leave even one Christian of that sort alive, if you let even one slip through the cracks, you're doomed. A Christian like that is the most powerful person on earth. A warrior for Christ who cannot be shamed into silence, cannot be intimidated, cannot be made to conform, cannot be controlled by earthly forces, is a nuclear bomb in God's holy arsenal. He is the sort of Christian who crushes empires and conquers civilizations. All you can do with such a man is kill him. He's too dangerous. Your tricks won't work. He has the grace of God, and you have nothing better to offer him.

Imagine if half of the alleged Christians in this country possessed half of the faith and courage of our brothers and sisters in Iraq or Somalia. Things would change overnight. Hollywood would crumble because we would refuse to watch its filth. The university system would be turned on its head because we would refuse to feed our children to it. The government would become a force of good, protecting innocent life and supporting the family, because we would refuse to vote for any politician who would support laws that undermine and destroy life and the family. We would wield our faith as a weapon against evil. We would cling to God. We would drink from His truth like a spring in the desert.

But we are too numb. Our faith is too stagnant, too stale, too watered-down, too wide. The great paradox of our religion is that the gate to eternal life is narrow, but God is larger than the cosmos itself. To get through the narrow gate, we must cling to that vast, eternal Being. If we cling instead to smaller things—our jobs, our relationships, our ambitions, our friends, our hobbies, our phones, our pets, or anything else—then we will not fit through the narrow passage. We will find ourselves on the broad path to destruction.

We are so firmly set on this ruinous path, many of us, that we don't even think of Him most of the time. We make little or no attempt to conform our lives to His commandments or to walk the narrow path that Christ forged for us. We are too busy for that. It's inconvenient. It's dull. Christ says, "Pick up your cross and follow Me," but we take it as a suggestion—just one possible way to live the Christian life. We leave our crosses on the side of the road and head back inside where it's warm and there's a new Netflix show to binge. We tell ourselves that we'll be fine in the end because we are decent people and we are leading normal lives, and God cannot penalize what is normal.

And Satan laughs.

He doesn't want us to be jolted out of this stupor. The persecutors of the church in America have quite an easy job. For them, the strategy is clear: Put down the gun. Drop the machete. Don't scare these people. Don't make martyrs of them. Don't give them any hint that there is a war going on and the fate of their souls hangs in the balance. Let them be arrogant and self-assured. Let them push out any thought of their own mortality. Let them dismiss everything I'm saying right now as "pessimistic" and "negative." Let them enjoy themselves. Let them snicker and laugh at anyone who actually takes his faith seriously. Let them whine about feeling judged—as if they are not being judged by the Eternal Judge every second of their lives. Let them dress up their spiritual indifference and cynicism as "positivity" and "hopefulness." Let them have it all. Fluff their pillow for them. Turn on the TV and hand them the remote. Feed them. Pamper them. Pleasure them. Comfort them. Lie to them. Give them every little thing their hearts desire. Don't appeal to their fear; appeal to their lust, their laziness, their gluttony, their vanity, their pride, their boredom. And watch them drop like flies into the fire.

Christ tells us the truth in clear and terrifying terms: "Enter through the narrow gate. For wide is the gate and broad is the road that leads to destruction, and many enter through it. But small is the gate and narrow the road that leads to life, and only a few find it" (Matthew 7:13–14).

Meaningless Battles

While Christianity is being destroyed from the inside, many Christians remain stationed at the perimeters, fighting skirmishes that have little meaning and no effect on the end result. You've heard, for example, of the alleged "War on Christmas." It is lamented that department store cashiers assault our ears with wishes of "Happy

Holidays" instead of "Merry Christmas." There are fights over manger scenes and Christmas lights. There was even a group of Christians (small, but vocal) enormously offended about a lack of Christmas graffiti on Starbucks cups a few years ago.[4]

It would seem that we still feel entitled to live in a Christmas wonderland filled with pretty lights and candy canes and stockings on the fireplace and Christmas music blaring from the overhead speakers at Walmart—even as we make no effort to actually live our faith at any other point of the year. We care deeply about preserving the fun stuff, but not about much else.

I wonder: How many of the people who whine about not hearing "Merry Christmas" have been inside a church on any day of the year that isn't December 24 or 25? Yet now they are suddenly so overcome with Christian fervor that they want even Home Depot to be adorned in religious decor? They could not be bothered to go to church and sing praises to the Lord at any time in the past fifty-two weeks, but now they want to hear praises to the Lord from the clerk at Sears?

Sure, there may be some devout and observant Christians who are deeply offended by "Happy Holidays." But I think they are few and far between, because, for one thing, serious Christians are likely to understand that "holiday" literally means "holy day." There is nothing secular about the phrase, actually. For another, the "War on Christmas" is a battle tailor-made for people who are too lazy to fight any other battle. It's an outrage the non-spiritual can indulge themselves in. It's an excuse for casual Christians to earn some easy points.

Here's the truth we must face: the church in America is not being killed from the outside. The secular, the non-Christian, even the Christian-haters are not destroying us. Christianity is not harmed in the slightest bit when some politically correct corporation bans Christmas decorations from its stores. Rather, the church is collapsing because of exactly the kinds of Christians who want Christmas but not Christianity. It is being destroyed not by unbelievers who refuse to acknowledge Christian holidays, but by believers who want the holidays and nothing else.

There are many other examples of these meaningless battles that we fight simply because we want to convince ourselves that we have not already lost the war. We desperately want to preserve and protect the religious decorations that still adorn our culture. We are horrified at attempts to erase "under God" from the Pledge of Allegiance and "in God we trust" from our currency. But why shouldn't those phrases be removed? *Are* we, actually, a nation that trusts God and places itself under His authority? If not, then why do we insist on bearing false witness? God has already been chased out of our society. We may as well let the relics of our religious past be swept aside as well. Perhaps then we will be forced to confront the deeper issue.

Strolling into Annihilation

We have been engaged in a decades-long campaign to widen the narrow road, even as we insist on decorating the road with religious paraphernalia. We have been walking along this broad path, and the Devil has gone in front of us, smoothing out every bump, clearing away the weeds, providing refreshments, and cheerfully encouraging us as we continue to stroll headfirst into annihilation. This is the great problem with American society: It is the widest gate the world has ever known. We are free to spread our arms and live exactly as we wish. But true freedom is not found in living exactly as we wish, but in living as God wishes.

We celebrate our "freedom"—which has become nothing more than the freedom to destroy ourselves. Our founders envisioned a people free to be moral and religious, enabled to achieve their full spiritual potential liberated from the oppression of a tyrannous government. We have taken this spiritual freedom and turned it into spiritual slavery. "You cannot serve two masters," Jesus warns. That means not just that we cannot serve two, but that we *will* serve one. No man is truly free to serve himself. He will either serve the God of Heaven or the Devil of Hell. Only the slave to Christ is free. The slave to Satan is wrung out like a sponge until he is nothing but a husk, and then the husk is incinerated.

The true danger we face is not cataclysmic and violent persecution, but the slow drifting from Truth. This is what has become of Christendom in the West. It caught a nice, warm wave and rode it into the darkness. Christians here are not falling away dramatically or suddenly. We are not disavowing God with hatred in our hearts. We are not even diving all the way into the depths of our sin, like the prodigal son, where we might hit the bottom and find ourselves sleeping in the mud with the pigs. We are not doing anything so decisive. We lack the conviction to even sin enthusiastically. We are not running away from God with determination. We are not running at all. Instead we have built a nice, comfortable raft of self-deception, and upon it we are floating gently, gently, gently into Hell.

CHAPTER THREE

Just Believe

*You believe that there is one God. Good! Even the demons
believe that—and shudder.*

—James 2:19

We have gotten ourselves on the wide road by widening Christianity itself. We have many ways of stretching and broadening our faith so that it no longer looks like anything or has any shape at all. And there is one word in particular that has assisted us in these efforts: belief. A modern Christian believes that believing he is a Christian is enough to make him a Christian. He thinks that his vague acknowledgment of God's reality and of Christ's saving work comes close enough to discipleship. He believes that belief is faith.

It is true that scripture uses the words "belief" and "faith" relatively interchangeably. "*Believe* in the Lord Jesus and you will be saved," Paul and Silas proclaim to the overwhelmed jailer in Acts 16:31. "Have *faith* in God" and you can move mountains, Our Lord tells His apostles in Mark 11:22. I think we can understand these as nearly identical exhortations. In Greek, belief and faith are variations of the word "pisteuo," which, significantly, is a verb. It is to put your full trust and confidence in something. In contemporary English, this is how most of us understand "faith." To have faith in God is not only to acknowledge His reality but to give yourself totally to Him. Faith is a complete investment and surrender of the self to God.

But our language does not treat "belief" the same way. If someone says he "believes" something, it means only that he accepts that it is probably true. Even if he says he "believes *in*" a thing, it could still only be an acknowledgement of its likely existence. For instance, you might say you "believe in" aliens. You would never say you "have faith in" aliens. Your belief in aliens is not a faith (unless you happen to be Tom Cruise). It is just a theory, a certain conditional confidence, that aliens are living somewhere out in the cosmos, scurrying about in hovercraft and doing whatever else aliens are supposed to do. When most Christians say they "believe in God," they mean it in essentially the same way, minus the hovercraft. They mean that they have given God their acknowledgment. They have made a spiritual gesture towards Him, as a sort of courtesy. They treat Him as you might treat a friendly acquaintance at a party, nodding to him from across the room and then hoping desperately that he doesn't come over to actually interact with you.

This is the problem with defining Christianity as "belief." The people in Paul's time knew what he meant when he told them to "believe in Lord Jesus." The people in our time do not have this understanding. They have been deceived, and allowed themselves to be deceived, by what Dietrich Bonhoeffer calls the doctrine of cheap grace: "Cheap grace is grace without discipleship, grace without the cross, grace without Jesus Christ, living and incarnate."[1] I might add that cheap grace is grace that treats Christ like a space alien: a being far off in the distance, somewhere beyond the clouds, speculative, mysterious, and irrelevant.

A Bridge over the Abyss

A religion of "belief" is a religion of passivity and speculation. It is a religion that requires no effort, no sacrifice, no personal involvement of any kind. It is a religion that only asks you to assent to the reality, or possibility, of a Divine Being. It features a God who asks only for your endorsement, like a politician running for office, a God who says, "Please give me your support"—and the support need only consist of putting a bumper sticker on your car. But this is not the Christian God. And the Christian who believes in such a God is not, by any meaningful measure, a Christian.

We are called to be not simply *believing* Christians, but *faithful* Christians. We must first believe, but we have not become truly Christian until we have graduated from that initial step to the next. I cannot put my faith in God—that is, I cannot surrender myself to Him and live in obedience to His divine will—unless I first accept the reality of His presence. But what if I accept the reality and yet do not surrender myself? What if I acknowledge that He is real, that He made all things, that He came into the world to rescue us from sin, but I categorically refuse to obey and submit? What if I accept His presence but not His commandments? What if I believe that He *is*, but I do not believe what He *says*? Then, as St. James observes, I am lower than an unbeliever. I am indeed in the same category as the demons. I have a knowledge of the one, true God, I admit that He is sovereign over all things, but I refuse to let Him exercise any influence over my life. I look to God and echo the words of Satan: *I will not serve.*

The West today is filled with this kind of Christian—these *believers.* They are like a man who walks up to a great abyss, notices a bridge stretching across it, and says, "Yes, well, there is a bridge. I believe in the presence of that bridge." And then, having given the bridge his full verbal endorsement, he retreats and sets up camp somewhere off in the distance, with the bridge barely in view. He will happily assent to the bridge's existence, but he will not walk across it. He knows that the bridge is there, but he will not trust it with his life. He will surrender his mind to the reality of the bridge, but he will not surrender his will. He will not put in any effort. He will not take any risk. And so he will never see the other side.

Jesus Christ is the bridge into eternal life. We cannot make it over the abyss just by staring at Him. We must give ourselves to Him. We must take one step onto the bridge, and then another, and then another. Our knees may shake and our legs may wobble, and we may fall and trip along the way, but we will never plunge into the depths so long as we cling tightly to the One who submitted to being trampled upon by man so that we could walk through Him into Paradise.

Faith in Motion

"Whoever believes in Him shall not perish but have eternal life" (John 3:16).[2] We tend to focus on the word "believe" in that verse while skipping over the word "in." We must put ourselves, through grace, *in* Christ. That is not a gesture of the intellect but an act of will. And it is a movement. We must move towards Him and into Him. The Christian life is truly a life, and life is motion. Everything that lives, moves. Stillness is a universal sign of death.

If we are to be living Christians, then we can never stay in one place. We are always traveling towards God—or else away from Him. To finally and completely reach God is to enter into Him, to live within Him in Heaven. But we will never arrive at that point in the course of our mortal existence. We can only get closer and closer to the end goal, or further and further from it. This is why Christ tells us repeatedly in scripture to "follow" Him. He does not tell us to stand beside Him, or sit, or lie on the ground near Him.

When Peter witnessed Christ in His glory at the Transfiguration, and saw Elijah and Moses appear with Him, he offered to pitch three tents for them. But it was not time for pitching tents. Elijah and Moses disappeared in an instant, and soon Our Lord and His three disciples were walking back down the mountain again. They were given a fleeting glimpse of glory. But it could not last. There was still so much to do.

"Follow me," says Our Lord. Keep moving. Keep going. The job is not yet done. Christ commands us to "be perfect" just as our Heavenly Father is perfect, knowing full well that we are not perfect, and in this life will never be. But we can strive toward perfection, toward holiness, toward home. That is what it means to have faith. Faith is in the striving, in the climbing, in the grasping for something we cannot yet see.

A man will make a thousand choices in a day. Nearly every choice moves him, by a few degrees, nearer to God or nearer to Hell. Of course, there is quite a lot of back and forth. He will cover the same ground again and again. He will move a mile closer to paradise and then leap backwards into the darkness. He will zig and zag and run forward and backpedal. If he is a faithful Christian, he will constantly recalibrate and correct himself. He will be converted again a hundred times. And though he continues to fail, he will also, over time, through God's grace, learn to swerve around certain potholes and avoid certain detours. His path will never be perfectly straight, but it will get straighter. He will never be sinless, but he will repent of his sins more sincerely, and each time get back on the road, headed in the right direction, with a renewed determination. There can be progress for a Christian, but there can never be, in this life, completion.

Most Christians today do not bother with spiritual progress. It is work, and they tell themselves that being a Christian should not require any work. They declare that they are fine in their current state, so they will kick up their feet and "trust in God." But trusting God is precisely the thing they are declining to do. After all, God told them to work out their salvation with fear and trembling. God told them to pick up their crosses and follow. God told them to obey the commandments. God told them to repent. God told them to give up everything. God told them to be chaste and humble and virtuous. God told them to die to the world. God told them to suffer and sacrifice and strive. They are not doing anything God told them to do. They are trusting in something, or someone, but it isn't God.

I said that the modern Christian reads "whoever believes in Him shall not perish" and overlooks the "in." But it turns out he doesn't take the verse seriously even without the "in." In that case it would read, "whoever believes Him shall not perish." Yet he doesn't believe God any more than he believes in God. For God told him to do many things he will not do, and not to do many things he is doing. Christ said, "You are my friends if you do what I command" (John 15:14). The modern Christian assumes that Christ was being hyperbolic and overly dramatic. Or else he assumes that he can get to Heaven even if he isn't a friend of Christ's. Both assumptions are catastrophically wrong.

It seems the contemporary interpretation of John 3:16 leaves out the word "in"—and every word after it. This beautiful declaration, which lies at the very foundation of our faith, has been sliced to pieces and reduced to two measly words: "Whoever believes." What you believe, and how you act on that belief, are now irrelevant considerations.

Incidental Christians

The issue is not *whether* we believe—believing is easy, especially if you don't think about it much. The question is rather: How *essential* is our belief to our lives? Is it just an incidental part or insignificant piece of the whole? Do we stuff Christ into a cramped little corner alongside old tennis rackets and camping supplies we've never used? Is Christianity sort of like a hobby, or a mild interest, or a contingency plan for a rainy day? This, I think, is how we have ended up as a "Christian" nation that looks, acts, and functions nothing like a Christian nation. It's because, while we have faith of a sort, that faith is incidental to our lives. It's just a part. Just one piece of the puzzle, no larger or more important than any other piece.

Once we've made something else a greater or equal priority to Christ in our lives, we'll find that Christ's share rapidly diminishes from that point on. If we decide to give him only a third of ourselves, or a quarter, or a tenth, He will forever struggle to reclaim the lost ground, but we, having relegated Him to third-wheel status, will fight against His efforts, seeing them as an intrusion. That's the thing about Jesus: He's either Lord and Savior and our only source of joy in this world, or He's a nuisance. If we are trying to find our purpose and our joy elsewhere, yet keep Christ around on retainer, we will find that He constantly interferes with our plans. We may think that we can put Him in sort of an advisory role, but He's not there just to advise us. He's not our cosmic life coach or our heavenly guidance counselor. Not merely, anyway. He wants us to submit totally to Him, and all of the "advice" He gives us points towards that end. If we are trying to avoid that end, then we will find ourselves striving more and more to decrease Christ within us.

The dominos fall pretty rapidly. Once we've trained our consciences to turn on and off, boxing Christ out of this or that little portion of our lives, it's relatively easy to repeat the process. Once you've made the conscious decision to create room in your life for some sin, even a small one, you've allowed Satan to establish a fortress in your heart. You've ceded some of your soul to him, even if it's just a tiny part of it. That's all he needs to begin his campaign to occupy, control, and finally destroy the whole thing.

It Is Finished

A Christian looking for an excuse to be spiritually sedentary will often point to the cross and remark, quite casually, that Christ has already done the work and there is nothing that we pitiful sinners could possibly do to supplement it or improve upon it. This is true, of course. But that truth does not mean what he thinks and hopes it means. It does not mean that the cross is some kind of hammock in which he can lie back with a glass of lemonade and watch the world go by. To treat it as such is not faith but rebellion.

Christ does not invite us to come and relax in the shade of His cross. When He said, "It is finished" (John 19:30), He did not mean that *our* work is finished. If that is what He meant, then why are we here? Did God send us into this dark and decaying world only so that we might offer Him our mental affirmation and then spend the rest of our lives waiting for the clock to run out? And if Christ requires nothing of us, then why does He require even so much as our affirmation? You cannot say, "There is nothing for us to do—it has all been done," and then say, "We must have faith." For faith *is* a thing we do. It is an act of the mind, the body, the soul. If I may be so bold as to dismiss five hundred years of agonizing and sometimes violent dispute, I actually don't see much of a conflict between "faith and works." I don't see why we are meant to choose between them or put one before the other. That would be like trying to decide whether love or fidelity is most important in a marriage. Fidelity is a dimension of marital love. You cannot separate them any more than you can separate one of the sides of a triangle from the other two sides. They are all a part of the same whole.

We cannot say that this or that action is enough to make a person Christian. But neither can we say that this or that thought, or this or that feeling, is enough to make a person Christian. Rather, our whole lives must be Christian. We must *be* Christian. Be is a verb. Being Christian is the act of living the Christian life. It cannot be divided into categories of thought and action. They are one, inexorably tied together. And in that oneness, in that unity between our Christian thoughts and our Christian feelings and our Christian actions, we find the essence of Christian faith.

It may be argued that these analogies to triangles and marriage only undermine my point. A man might have fidelity to his wife, he might remain loyal and honest, and yet have no love for her—just so, a Christian may act like a Christian and perform Christian works, and yet have no or little faith. Is not love greater than loyalty, and faith greater than work? Is a triangle not greater than one of its sides by itself? Yes, I think so. You can have loyalty without love, a side without a triangle, and work without faith. But it doesn't work the other way. You can't have love without loyalty, a triangle without one of its sides, or faith without work. The whole is greater than its parts, but it cannot exist without its parts. And the parts are not mere symbols of the whole. They are indeed parts. The *act* of faith, the work, springs from the internal life of faith within a person. A faith that exists only inside and not without, a faith that has no act, no expression, no work, is dead.

Those who emphasize only the internal experience of faith create a problem I have rarely heard anyone in their camp address. Consider a man who may be going through a period of spiritual dryness or doubt. Perhaps he fears his faith is waning. Perhaps he feels himself tormented by the "dark night of the soul" that St. John of the Cross describes. Should he now cease all religious activity? Should he stop living and acting as a Christian because he no longer feels like one?

No, of course not. He should remain on the same external path. He should continue, if not double down on, the "work" of Christianity. Some may say he is now "going through the motions," and this is true, but the motions are far from empty. They are maybe more meaningful now than they've ever been before, precisely because he gains no spiritual comfort or fulfillment through them. It is best if the activity of faith flows from our inner experience of faith, but if we are in turmoil, and our souls are lost in a desert of spiritual dryness, then the process may have to work backwards for a time. We may have to rely on our actions to ignite and animate our inner faith, instead of the other way around. A man who feels no love for his wife would be well advised to do the same. He must act like he loves her, he must live like it, until the feeling returns. And it probably will return, unless he allows his actions to express his inner lack of love just as they once expressed his inner abundance of love. In that case, his marriage might be ruined.

John Henry Newman defines faith this way: "To surrender one's self to God, humbly to put one's interests, or to wish to be allowed to put them, into His hands who is the Sovereign Giver of all good."[3] Or we can use Bonhoeffer's definition: "When Christ calls a man, He bids Him come and die."[4] By both definitions, there is an inner and outer experience. A mental, emotional, and physical surrender is necessary. Christ invites us to the same glorious fate as the penitent thief on Calvary. He invites us to die beside Him so that we may live forever in Him. If we are to die to ourselves, we must do it with every part and facet of ourselves, intellectually and physically, internally and externally. Anyone who wishes to have faith in his mind but not with his actions, or to have faith with his actions but not with his mind, does not wish to have faith at all. Such a person seeks to be a half-Christian, a hybrid, a monstrosity. He wishes to cut himself into pieces and give one part to the world and the other to God. But God does not want just a chunk of him. He wants the whole thing.

Faithful Disobedience?

I think our real objective, when we settle for belief rather than faith and intellectual assent rather than self-surrender, is simply to avoid the challenges of obedience. These days we sneer at the very notion of obedience and treat a Christian who strives for obedience as a primitive relic of a less enlightened spiritual age. We will even say that his focus on obedience is a sign of his *lack* of faith. A Christian with true faith, we pretend, is one who would never deign to insult Jesus by taking His prescriptions seriously. A true Christian knows that Christ died for his sin, and so he can continue sinning, confident that the wages for his future misdeeds have already been paid. We treat the atonement as a blank check and an excuse for self-indulgence.

This attitude has no relationship to the gospel. Jesus tells us, "If you love me, keep my commandments" (John 14:15). Again: "If you want to enter life, keep the commandments" (Matthew 19:17). He does not suggest keeping the commandments as a token of our appreciation. He says that faith and obedience are linked. Obedience is an element of faith.

The de-emphasis of obedience is a terrible thing because it is a de-emphasis of Christ's very life. We tend to focus almost exclusively on the Crucifixion and Resurrection, forgetting that a whole life was lived before that point, and a whole religion worth of teachings was imparted to us during that time. It is true that Easter is the holiest Christian holiday because it celebrates the Resurrection, but can we really say that the Incarnation was less important? The Resurrection could not have happened without it. Can we really say that any event in Christ's life, any particular moment, was less important than any other? I don't think it's possible to divide His life into episodes and rank each one according to importance. It is all a part of one whole, and the whole, His life, is utterly and eternally necessary to us.

So why would He waste His time telling us how to live if we need not live that way? Why would He leave us holy scripture if almost everything it contains is now effectively moot? Why would He preach and teach for three years before His sacrifice if those teachings were then made useless by the sacrifice itself?

Thomas Aquinas taught that Christ could have redeemed all mankind with one single drop of His precious blood. We could have been saved, then, by His circumcision. We could have been saved early in His ministry if He had allowed the angry mob to toss Him off a cliff. We could have been saved if He had submitted to being stoned to death by the Pharisees. We could have been saved at any time, and in any manner, that God chose.

Yet the cross was, in some mysterious way, the most fitting method for our redemption, and He surrendered Himself to it when the most fitting time had arrived. Why that time and not earlier? We cannot completely comprehend the answer to that question, but I think we can know part of it: He did not die sooner because He still had more to tell us. His missionary work was not complete. There were things we *needed* to know. A way of life we *needed* to adopt.

"Whoever wants to be my disciple must deny themselves and take up their cross and follow me" (Matthew 16:24). I do not think Christ wasted any time or any words. He chose them all with perfect wisdom. So when He says that His disciples "must" do this, He really means "must." There is no other way. No differing approach. It is not that He would *prefer* for His disciples to deny themselves and follow Him. It is that a person who will not do those things *cannot be* a disciple. A disciple, by nature, is one who follows and obeys. And only a person of this kind, possessing this nature, can exist in Heaven.

There is one other thing that should be noted about our moral obligations: they are pretty easy, all things considered. It is all the more pitiful that we go to such great lengths to get around our duties, considering how light the burden actually is. It may seem difficult in the moment—I know it certainly does for me—but, when put in perspective, all God is really asking of us is a bit of patience and a bit of discipline. I'm reminded of that great scene from Graham Greene's *The Power and the Glory*, when his protagonist priest, a coward and a drunkard for most of the novel, is awaiting his martyrdom in a Mexican jail. While contemplating his impending demise, he has a revelation:

> [H]e was not at the moment afraid of damnation—even the fear of pain was in the background. He felt only an immense disappointment because he had to go to God empty-handed, with nothing done at all. It seemed to him at that moment that it would have been quite easy to have been a saint. It would only have needed a little self-restraint, and a little courage. He felt like someone who has missed happiness by seconds at an appointed place. He knew now that at the end there was only one thing that counted—to be a saint.[5]

Just a little self-restraint, a little courage. That's all it takes. And it's really not very much for God to ask, considering all He has done for us.

The Greatest Commandment

But the question still lingers: Why couldn't Our Lord punch all our tickets to Heaven so that nothing else was required of us? Why did Jesus give us all of these instructions if He was just going to redeem us anyway? What is the point of the Sermon on the Mount and the parables and the Ten Commandments? Why wasn't all of that negated by the atonement?

I think we can come to see the answer to those questions if we look beyond belief, and even faith, and towards what St. Paul calls the greatest of all: love. The point of our existence, the whole reason we were sent here, is to love God. Love is an act of the will, a choice, not the fruit of compulsion or force. Whatever God can do for me, He will do and has done. Still, He cannot force me to love Him. He can give me the grace to love Him. He can set me on the path towards loving Him. He can love me with all the force of eternity and give me all the tools in the universe that I could possibly need. But I must love Him. I must *consent* to love, as Scott Hahn has said.[6] There can be no love without consent. And there cannot be that ultimate completion of love, the completion that is eternal life, unless God's love for me is reciprocated, even if faintly and imperfectly.

In *The Great Divorce*, C. S. Lewis describes the souls of Hell as thin, evaporating entities who literally cannot exist in Heaven because they lack the substance necessary to survive there.[7] Pulling a soul out of Hell and plopping it into Heaven would be like digging a worm out of the ground and letting him bake in the summer sun. The very fire that gives light and warmth to the heavenly regions would reduce the poor creature to shriveled ash. A worm is not substantial enough to live on the surface of the earth, and the completely self-absorbed souls of the damned are not substantial enough for Heaven.

It is through loving God that I develop the substance that will fit me for Heaven. By choosing to accept His love, my very nature changes and I become not the sort of person who *deserves* to enter Heaven—not one of us deserves to—but the sort of person who *can* enter it. There can be nothing but love there. If I have no love for God, no matter how much He has for me, how can I pass through the gates? If I have not allowed His love to penetrate into my core, into my will, if I have not surrendered myself to it, then there is nothing in me that can exist in that place. I am a being of selfishness and hate, a being of nothingness. There is nowhere for me to go but into the dark.

A God in Hiding

I think, by the way, that this explains why God remains mostly invisible in this world. Atheists often claim that God does not exist because if He did, He would surely appear before us in the sky, reveal Himself in His glory, and put to rest all of our doubts and misgivings. I must say that I have thought the same thing in my life at different points. And if all God wanted was our "belief," then I'm sure He would do exactly that. In fact, it would be cruel for Him to remain hidden if belief and belief alone could get us to the Promised Land.

But God wants our love, and we cannot love without making the choice to do so. He must therefore remain out of view for now, revealing Himself in indirect ways, mostly working within the chain of natural cause and effect, speaking to us in our hearts but not audibly, because that is the only environment in which choice is possible. Standing in His presence, looking upon Him, all choice would melt away. We would be too overcome with fear and awe, too stupefied, too astonished, to develop in that moment the quiet and humble love that He desires from us. Christ found only three in His company who could bear to witness His divine glory at the Transfiguration, and then only for a moment, and only after they had given their lives to Him. In this life, you and I will never witness such a scene. It is good that we don't witness it. It would overwhelm and overpower our will, making true love impossible.

Christ brought us everything we need to develop that love. He gave salvation and hope and light. He did everything for us that He possibly could. He carried the world on His back all the way up Calvary. There is only one step we must take—and not alone, and not without grace, but still we must take it. We must love. And His ministry on earth was meant to teach us about love. He told us what it consists of, what it does, how it thinks, how it acts, how it lives. The greatest commandment is to love God with our whole selves. All other commandments are contained in that one. That is why we must follow them. That is what Jesus taught. And after He taught us about love, and described it to us in great detail, He picked up the cross, walked up that hill, and demonstrated.

CHAPTER FOUR

My Buddy Jesus

*Therefore, since we are receiving a kingdom that cannot be
shaken, let us be thankful, and so worship God acceptably
with reverence and awe.*

—Hebrews 12:28

W e have used Christ's humility against Him. In only one chapter of the gospel, John 15, Our Lord pays us the unthinkable compliment of calling us His friends. It is an expression of supreme humility on His part, and all the more reason for us to fall at His feet in gratitude and worship. But we have latched onto this description—ignoring the more numerous instances in scripture where we are called children, servants, slaves, and sheep—to extrapolate a new and quite flattering interpretation of our status in the order of things. It is like we have conflated "friend" with "peer."

I might say that I am a friend to my children, but I don't mean it as a statement of democratic equality, nor do I intend to deemphasize my authority over them. I mean it as an expression of intimacy and closeness. I am their friend because I care for them and have their best interests at heart. This does not make them my peers. My son would be in for a severe scolding if he ever introduced me to his friends as "My buddy Matt." I am always Dad first, not a buddy, and it is for the greater good of the family that my paternal office is ever recognized and respected.

In the same way, Jesus calls us His friends because He cares for us and wants us to gain a more intimate knowledge of Him. He is not "My buddy Jesus." He is "My King, My Lord, My God." We should always approach Him with reverence, obedience, and awe, which are probably not qualities present in our earthly friendships. That is because our friendship with Christ is nothing at all like our earthly friendships.

The Hangout Jesus

It is often said that Jesus "hung out with sinners" or "hung out with prostitutes" during His earthly ministry. There's more wrong with this than the scandalously irreverent phrasing. The point is to slander Christ the same way the Pharisees slandered Him, to make it seem as if Our Lord was one of them, and that he tolerated, accepted, even embraced their behavior. That is what "hanging out" entails. We speak of Jesus this way because we want to bring Him down to our level. We would rather shape Christ than be shaped by Christ. It is easier to drag Him into the muck with us than to climb up that hill, up Calvary, to meet Him. James and John arrogantly asked to sit at Christ's right and left in His Kingdom. But at the cross, it was two thieves at His right and left—the one time when Jesus really did hang with sinners, and for them. One of them would enter into His Kingdom that very day, but he had to die first.

A man who learns about Jesus by listening to what our culture says about Him will most likely come away with the mental picture of an apathetic hippie who wandered around Galilee flanked by drunks and hookers. He will imagine Our Lord sitting on the side of the road making small talk and watching the world pass by. Ultimately, he will come to the conclusion that Christ was a sheep, not a shepherd. And this is the conclusion that those who talk about Christ "hanging out" mean for him to draw. It is why they choose the phrase "hung out with" rather than a more accurate description such as "taught" or "ministered to."

Yes, it's true that Christ ate with social outcasts and came to their defense against judgmental religious hypocrites. Yes, He did so in defiance of social customs and to the chagrin of the Jewish upper class, who were scandalized by the whole spectacle. But He had a reason for doing this, and it was not merely to "hang out." Nor was it an expression of any sort of romanticized idea of the lower classes. He was not a hippie or a Robin Hood. He came to the sinners as a doctor, to treat their sickness (Mark 2:17). Not merely to "accompany them," as Pope Francis likes to say. That is why He said "Sin no more" to the adulteress (John 8:11). And it is why He proclaimed that salvation had come to the publican Zacchaeus's house only *after* Zacchaeus had promised to pay back any money he had stolen and give half his possessions to the poor (Luke 19:1–10). He did not come to the adulteress to approve of her adultery, or to the tax collector to approve of his greed and corruption. He came to purge them of their sins—and us of ours. That is what His friendship means. We must remember that the sinners Christ befriended in scripture did not hang around Him idly, content in their ways. Rather, they fell before Him weeping, and bathed His feet with their tears.

A Casual Congregation

I think it is partly due to our perverse, self-centered understanding of Christ's friendship that our faith has become such a casual and easygoing affair. We stroll up to the divine mysteries and look upon them with jaded familiarity. We treat Jesus like a drinking buddy or an old high school friend. Walk into most churches in America and you will see this attitude on full display. Indeed, if you knew nothing of Christianity and happened to wander into one of these buildings, you'd be forgiven for assuming that the congregants are members of some sort of social club. There would be little in their demeanor, their dress, their conduct, or the service to suggest that the people were gathering to worship the Author of all Creation.

Reverence and sacredness have been drained out of church, starting with the buildings themselves. I will never forget the time my wife and I accidentally attended a non-denominational megachurch because we thought it was a mall. The coffee stand and gift shop in the lobby didn't immediately clarify the situation. Someone had to actually tell us, "You are in a church." For all the lights and noises and fanfare, it seemed that the congregants were actually quite shy about the fact that they were worshipping God.

In the old days, Christians wanted their churches to be beautiful. Now we go out of our way to make sure our churches are not beautiful, lest the beauty give anyone the uncomfortable impression that God is present. Some Catholic parishes have been engaged in an active process of uglifying their houses of worship, taking down old artwork and disposing of the statues that once adorned the sanctuary. It is not just Joel Osteen who has decided he wants no reminders or symbols of Jesus distracting the congregation from the more serious business of listening to the opinions of the pastor. Many churches have adopted a similar approach. Take, for instance, the Baptist church in South Carolina that recently removed a hand-carved statue of Jesus that certain members of the congregation found upsetting to their sensibilities.[1]

But, of course, the décor matters little as long as the service itself is conducted with the utmost reverence and respect. Sadly, however, the blandness and ugliness of the physical building will often be met and exceeded by what is actually happening in it: People milling about in flip-flops and shorts, chatting loudly in the lobby and in the pews. A jeans-clad church band playing music too hokey to be secular but too secular to be sacred. A pastor who gives a sermon that sounds like a pep talk from a high school guidance counselor. And there will be noise. Always noise. Every second of "worship" accompanied by noise. Never a moment of solemn silence. Never a moment of contemplation.

The modern churchgoing experience is marked by its lack of reverence. It does not give a hint of anything sacred or mystical. There is nothing that forces the reality and presence of God into your mind. Church has become an extension of secular culture rather than an antidote to it. Jesus tells us that He is present in a special way when Christians gather together in His name. Should this incredible fact not be reflected in every aspect of our worship?

Consider how the figures of scripture react when in the presence of the divine. Relating his vision of God, Isaiah paints a picture that makes a stark contrast to the casual, chatty, coffee-drinking scene in most churches today:

> I saw the Lord sitting on a throne, high and lofty; and the hem of his robe filled the temple. Seraphs were in attendance above him; each had six wings: with two they covered their faces, and with two they covered their feet, and with two they flew. And one called to another and said:
> "Holy, holy, holy is the Lord of hosts; the whole earth is full of his glory."

The pivots on the thresholds shook at the voices of those who called, and the house filled with smoke. And I said: "Woe is me! I am lost, for I am a man of unclean lips, and I live among a people of unclean lips; yet my eyes have seen the King, the Lord Almighty!" (Isaiah 6:1–5)

There is smoke and thunder, and a great throne upon which sits the Lord of Hosts. The angels attending Him—seraphim, the highest created beings in the celestial hierarchy—will not look upon His face or touch the ground where His throne sits. Isaiah, seeing this, cries out in fear and awe.

When Jesus appeared to John to give His revelation, John "fell at His feet as though dead" (Revelation 1:17). Peter had a similar reaction when he first witnessed one of Christ's miracles: "He fell at Jesus' knees and said, 'Go away from me, Lord; I am a sinful man!'" (Luke 5:8) All through the Holy Book we read of people being brought to their knees in reverence and adoration upon encountering the supernatural reality of God. So what can we say about the almost complete lack of reverence and adoration in our churches? What can we say about the people who saunter lackadaisically into His presence, not having bothered to dress for the occasion and without stopping for even a moment of silent meditation?

They are either prideful to an impossible degree, or they do not really consider themselves to be in God's presence—they are not really thinking about God much at all. For the sake of charity, I will assume the latter explanation. In fact, I need not assume it. I have been guilty of displaying this casual attitude myself in church on many occasions, and it is always because I have not paused to seriously contemplate the sacred act in which I am partaking. It is easy not to contemplate it, as most churches are designed to interfere with such contemplation.

A couple of years ago I was personally attacked—that's how it felt, anyway—during a sermon at a church in Pennsylvania while I was on vacation. The priest was speaking about this very topic: the need for reverence and respect in worship. He admonished the congregation because many of the men couldn't even be bothered to put on long pants and a nice shirt, and some of the women had come dressed like they just stumbled out of a college bar at 2:00 a.m. (my phrasing, not his). The pastor explained that the lackadaisical, slovenly attire was a symptom of a far greater problem—many Christians have a lackadaisical, slovenly spiritual life. Their outfits only reflect that fact.

I say that I felt personally attacked because, as I listened, I looked down and remembered that I was wearing a T-shirt and shorts. And flip-flops, God forgive me. Oh, I had a reasonable explanation. I hadn't remembered to pack formal attire, you see. I began to feel quite angry at the priest for making this sweeping statement without considering that some of us might have a good reason to be dressed like beach bums. I knew I'd have to walk down the aisle like a scolded schoolboy, wearing exactly what I had just been told not to wear. I was offended. I had an excuse, and it was outrageous that this guy hadn't prefaced his remarks by exempting me, personally, from everything he was about to say. How dare he assume that I lack reverence just because I was wearing pool clothes to church?

But I couldn't convince myself. He was right. I had no excuse. I had been chastised, and I deserved to be. As I thought about it, I understood that this isolated incident was not so isolated. I often lack the appropriate reverence and humility when approaching God in church or in prayer or in any situation. There is little of the solemn and the sacred in my faith life, I conceded. He nailed it: this wardrobe malfunction was a symptom of a deeper problem. I left that day resolved to do better, and, though I still am far from perfect in this or any other regard, I believe I have improved, by the grace of God.

Sure, I could have stormed out of church, my sandals flapping furiously as I walked, and never come back. I could have whined about that mean "judgmental" man who had the audacity to criticize my behavior. I could have been so offended that I left the faith entirely and never returned. I could have spent the rest of my life telling stories, as people often do, about the self-righteous old puritan who caused me to leave Christianity, through no fault of my own. But had I gone that route, it would have been no great loss to the church. If I am going to be scared away by a little light admonishment, I was never much of a Christian to begin with.

But reverence is about more than church attire. And the lack of reverence among Christians creates serious problems outside the walls of any church building. It becomes a scandal because it causes the unbeliever to justifiably doubt the seriousness of our beliefs—and thus to doubt the legitimacy of our claims. He can look at us in church, or anywhere else, and see that we ourselves do not appear to be operating as if a Most High Judge is watching and guiding us. In most cases an atheist will have more reason to take Islam seriously, because Muslims appear to take Islam seriously. A Muslim who prays five times a day, lying prostrate on the ground, is acting like a person would act if he actually believed in his God. A Christian who rarely prays at all, and never on his knees, and goes to church mostly to socialize, and never displays anything like reverence in church or outside of it, is acting like a person would act if he didn't actually believe in his God at all. And if the Christian doesn't believe it, thinks the atheist, why should he?

American Idol

There is one more point to be made on this topic of reverence. I cannot help but notice a strange dichotomy in the thinking of many

conservative Christians in this country. They often have much more reverence for America and its symbols than for God and His. Most conservative Christians demand that the flag be approached with sacred awe, treated with extreme adoration, and handled as though it is the Ark of the Covenant. They insist on a certain posture when facing the flag. Songs must be sung to it. Tribute must be paid. Stand. Hand on heart. Follow the choreography. To sit during the anthem is akin to blasphemy.

Now, I quite agree that the flag should be given respect. I will stand with my hand on my heart and sing (quietly, for the sake of surrounding ears). To desecrate or burn the flag is, in my view, an act of loathsome disrespect. But America should not be our God. The flag should not be our cross. They are temporal things, doomed to eventual decay and non-existence. Countries come and go. Flags are flown and then relegated to museums. That is the way of the world. We should not esteem temporal things over eternal things. And if we insist on hushed veneration during a color guard presentation, reverent participation during the singing of the anthem, proper postures and hand gestures in the presence of the flag, and devout and respectful handling of that flag, then how could we not insist on reverence to an exponentially greater degree when it comes to the things and symbols and rituals of God?

Over the past few years many evangelical pastors have come out strongly against NFL players kneeling during the national anthem. Megachurch pastor Robert Jeffress once said those players are doing something "absolutely wrong" and they should be grateful not to have to worry about "being shot in the head for taking a knee" as they would be in North Korea.[2] I agree with Pastor Jeffress that kneeling for the anthem is wrong. My children would certainly be in a lot of trouble if they ever disrespected the flag the way those players did.

Still, I wonder: Has Pastor Jeffress ever denounced the lack of reverence in Christian worship in terms nearly so severe? Does he

think that your posture in front of the flag is more important than your posture and demeanor at church or during prayer or when approaching the divine mysteries at any other time? I can understand the argument that reverence isn't necessary in any context. I disagree with that argument, but I understand it. I do not understand the argument that reverence is necessary in patriotic matters but not religious matters. That seems to me like idol worship.

A Personal Relationship

The casual and "friendly" approach to faith will most commonly be justified with the claim that Christianity is supposed to be a "personal relationship with Jesus." I have come to dislike this phrase, though there is nothing on the surface wrong with striving for a personal relationship with Jesus. In one sense, a personal relationship is exactly what we should have. Our relationship to God and with Him should indeed be a relationship, in that it should be marked by intimacy, affection, and understanding. But the great Christians of the past had no use for this "personal relationship" language. They would have been confused by it, even though the Christianity of those times was far more intimate, and far more personal, than most of what we see in the church today. Consider how St. Augustine writes to God in his *Confessions*:

> Late have I loved you, beauty so old and so new; late have I loved you. And see, you were within and I was in the external world and sought you there, and in my unlovely state I plunged into those lovely created things which you made. You were with me, and I was not with you. The lovely things kept you far from me, though if they did not have their existence in you, they had no existence at all.

You called and cried out loud and shattered my deafness. You were radiant and resplendent, you put to flight my blindness. You were fragrant, and I drew in my breath and now pant after you. I tasted you, and I feel but hunger and thirst for you. You touched me, and I am set on fire to attain the peace which is yours.[3]

Nobody can accuse Saint Augustine of having a faith suffocated by formality. The modern Christian cannot conceive of so intimate and relatable a God—he cannot think of God in terms so personal. Yet it is precisely the modern Christian who has invented the phrase "my personal relationship with Jesus." Why has the phrase gained popularity while the actual thing itself has become obsolete?

I think the answer lies in emphasis. Very often, the man who cites his personal relationship with Jesus—usually defensively, when his lethargic approach to faith is called into question—will say, "Well, this is *my* personal relationship with Jesus." Emphasis on "my." He thinks that this relationship is something he himself owns. He directs it and defines it. He calls the shots. He wants the relationship to be his in the same way that a neglectful husband wants the marriage to be his. He is the star of the show, and his needs and preferences always reign supreme.

He takes his cue not from scripture but from the theological ruminations of Depeche Mode: "Your own personal Jesus / Someone to hear your prayers / Someone who cares."[4] In his mind, Jesus has become an invisible genie that he carries around in his pocket. When he prays at all, he prays to a deity he has invented for himself. He worships a God who worships him.

But we will not grow closer to Jesus this way. If we want a real relationship with Him, we must find it in *Him*. We must look away from ourselves and into the Divine Truth. We cannot develop a relationship with God by plunging deeper into the abyss of our own egos. Intimacy with God is forged in surrender and obedience, in denial of self. We can only have a real relationship with Him if we remember that that relationship is between Creator and created, King and subject, Father and child. We cannot connect with God or know Him except on those terms.

The Secular Tide

Our casual, false, and self-serving approach to faith has resulted in disaster. Christ has been ripped from the center of human existence and sent out to the hinterlands. It is hard enough for mortal, selfish men to feel the presence of an invisible God. It is even harder today—perhaps harder than it has ever been in history—because there is little sign or mention of Him in our secular society. We have built what Charles Taylor in *A Secular Age* calls "buffered selves." Between ourselves and God lies a giant buffer that obscures the mystical light of divinity. We can break through this barricade—a barricade consisting of material possessions, jobs, relationships, the internet, media, and every other thing—but to break through it we must do more than shrug casually at God.[5]

A reverent and devoted faith is militant, aggressive. It relentlessly pursues God and rejects with great prejudice all that does not come from Him. This sort of aggression is what is needed in these times. Anything less, and we will be swept up in the secular tide and washed into a life of doubt and unbelief. The consequence of living in a secular age is that secularism is the default setting. You must try very hard to live and think as a Christian, or else you will naturally, by force of cultural gravity, find yourself living and thinking as an atheist.

Our ancestors built and lived in a Christian civilization where Christianity was seamlessly interwoven into every facet of existence.

Everything was a sign of God's presence. Everything was a religious affair. There was no life outside of faith. There was no wall separating the church from everything else. Our civilization, on the other hand, has erected a wall so high that it takes great effort just to remember that there is a God over on the other side of it. Our everyday experience often feels profoundly disconnected from any sort of spiritual reality. And this is why reverence and devotion have never been more important. They remind us that there is something beyond this fog and this dark. They're like a lighthouse, showing us that we are not drifting forever in a black sea. There is land, however far in the distance it may be.

As I close this chapter, I want to offer a brief word of encouragement to anyone who struggles to feel God's presence in this godless atmosphere. It is quite easy, as I said, to forget about God altogether in a world filled with TV shows, advertisements, social media, shopping malls, cars, billboards, gossip, pettiness, and all of the defining features of modern life, which are so small and superficial yet so numerous and intrusive as to block our view of eternity.

Someone recently told me that he believes in God, but, he confessed, "It doesn't *feel* like He is real." I understand this feeling. When you are walking through a Walmart, or scrolling through Facebook, or watching a sitcom on television, you will not often feel the reality and presence of God surging into your mind. I think that is part of the reason why we like to spend so much of our time doing those things. It must be granted that in those moments—which comprise almost all of our waking moments—God feels too extraordinary, too immense, too supernatural to be real. It is easy to get bogged down in the minutiae of daily life and begin to see God as a fantastic, unbelievable myth.

But consider this: In those moments, does it "feel like" there are two trillion galaxies in the universe? Does it feel like space is filled with planets, stars, black holes, and a billion other marvels? Does it feel like dinosaurs once roamed the earth? Does it feel like the pyramids are real? Does it feel like ancient Rome ever existed? While you are sitting in traffic, can you "feel" the depths of the ocean, or the immensity of the rain forest, or the complexity of the human brain? Nobody denies the existence of any of these things, yet we do not feel like we live in a world awesome enough to include them. But we do.

We know, and even the atheist will admit, that reality consists of many wonders that seem too fantastic to be real, too good to be true, too marvelous to actually be a part of our mundane and tedious reality. There is a reason why it's hard to believe in God in the supermarket checkout line, but not hard at all under the night sky. Perhaps the answer is to spend more time under the sky, and less time in the checkout line.

CHAPTER FIVE

The Gospel of Positivity

Though he slay me, yet will I hope in him.

—Job 13:15

W e all want to be happy. It is the most natural and instinctive of human desires. But the deepest and realest happiness—that state we call joy—cannot be attained without a certain amount of pain and discomfort. Joy removed from the cross, joy that denies or ignores the cross, joy that wants the Resurrection apart from the Crucifixion, is a false joy. It is not joy at all but mere optimism. "Positivity," as we call it today. Many millions are led happily astray by this bundle of cheap hope and ignorant bliss.

The Gospel of Positivity is everywhere in our culture—preached from the pulpit, extolled on television, celebrated in popular songs and movies. It can be detected in subtler forms whenever one Christian rebukes another for speaking seriously about sin, Hell, death, suffering, or some other challenging topic. He labels such talk "fire and brimstone," or "pessimistic"—and calls any discussion of morality "Puritanism." Then he goes whistling on his merry way, sure that he has banished the difficult facts of human existence by banishing any vocal acknowledgment of those facts.

But sometimes the Gospel of Positivity is subtler that that. Consider the sort of Christian who cannot manage to sit down and read the Bible without taking a beautifully staged picture and putting it on Instagram or Facebook: the Bible on a table next to a coffee mug, with a smoldering fireplace in the background. A person holding the Bible as he looks out over a beach at sunset, or a peaceful mountain, or a flowery field. The Bible on someone's lap with only her comfortable, brightly colored socks and café mocha in view. As I write these words, I am looking at a picture like this on one of my social media feeds. A woman has posted an image of her Bible, carefully highlighted and dog-eared, next to a ripe grapefruit and a plate of scrambled eggs with garnish. "My usual breakfast," the caption reads. But somehow I doubt she reads the Bible at breakfast every day, just as I doubt that she garnishes her scrambled eggs every day.

The point of these pictures is primarily to announce to the world that the picture-taker is reading the Bible. It is the modern equivalent of standing on the street corner and praying like a hypocrite—something that Jesus warned against in the Sermon on the Mount. And the message we take from these pictures, whether or not we mean to take it this way, is that the Christian life is a trendy and scenic sort of thing. We expect that when we pick up the Bible we will immediately feel the same peaceful relaxation that the Instagram Christian does. What we don't realize is that the Instagram Christian is too busy using his Bible as a prop to actually open it and read it. If he feels any peace and relaxation, it is because he is on the beach or looking at a mountain or sitting in front of a fireplace. It has nothing to do with the Bible at all.

The Helpless Estate

The Christian music and movie industries have made millions peddling this kind of Christianity. Considered on its own, in a vacuum, any particular Christian radio hit or "faith-based film" seems harmless enough, even edifying. But the whole mass of it all together, the Christian entertainment industry as a whole, gives us a sleek, cheery, safe, unchallenging image of God and faith. It is Christianity run through a filtration system where all of the sorrow and sin and the basic realities of everyday life are filtered out. It is Christianity packaged for mass consumption.

Christian pop music, in particular, is popular because it is cheery and inoffensive. Christians appreciate it, for good reason, because it lacks the vulgarity and nihilism common in secular music. But too often it also lacks depth, character, and artistry. It fails to convey pain, sorrow, or desperation. A Christian song must always have an upbeat feel and end on a happy note. Every song must be Easter. There can never be a Good Friday.

Consider these lyrics from the song "Nobody Loves Me Like You" by the popular Christian artist Chris Tomlin:

> Morning, I see you in the sunrise every morning
> It's like a picture that You've painted for me
> A love letter in the sky [. . .]
> Nobody loves me like you love me Jesus
> I stand in awe of your amazing ways. . . .[1]

These words express a very nice sentiment—though they are utterly indistinguishable from the lyrics of about a million other Christian pop songs. You could throw words like "amazing," "Jesus," and "love" into a cocktail shaker and pour out this stuff ad nauseam.

But the real trouble is that all we ever get from Christian artists is nice sentiments like these. Rarely do they grapple seriously with pain and sorrow.

It is painfully clichéd, but in a sense true, that the morning sunrise is a "love letter in the sky" from God, but most people do not wake up every day feeling that way. Indeed, some people are so deeply in pain that they dread the dawn of each new day. What do the Christian artists have to say to those people? They used to have quite a lot to say.

Horatio Spafford was a nineteenth-century hymnist. His son died at the age of two. A fire destroyed his business. All four of his daughters drowned in a shipwreck. It was after that last tragedy that Spafford sat down and channeled his unspeakable pain into a song called "It Is Well with My Soul":

> When peace like a river attendeth my way,
> When sorrows like sea billows roll,
> Whatever my lot, thou hast taught me to say
> It is well, it is well, with my soul.
>
> It is well
> With my soul
> It is well, it is well with my soul.
>
> Though Satan should buffet, though trials should come,
> Let this blest assurance control,
> That Christ has regarded my helpless estate,
> And hath shed His own blood for my soul.
>
> It is well (it is well)
> With my soul (with my soul)

It is well, it is well with my soul.

My sin, oh, the bliss of this glorious thought
My sin, not in part but the whole,
Is nailed to the cross, and I bear it no more,
Praise the Lord, praise the Lord, O my soul.

Not only are these words far more eloquent. They deal seriously with suffering and misery—with the "helpless estate," as Spafford calls it, of being human. The Gospel of Positivity cannot produce a hymn like this because it refuses to grapple with that reality.

The Christian movie industry isn't any better in this regard. Generally, "faith-based" films tend to be emotionally manipulative, theologically suspect, morally compromised, and highly embarrassing on a number of levels. That doesn't stop them from turning massive profits, of course. There is a lot of money to be made in Christian entertainment because the audience cares less about quality than about having their own beliefs repeated back to them. No need to spend money and time producing something with depth or insight or artistic value. Just hit the right notes, repeat the right lines, pander in the right way, and you'll make millions. This is not a good state of affairs—it makes Christians look shallow to the outside world, and, worse, it causes Christians to actually *become* shallow because their religious ideas are being shaped by cheap emotionalism.

Many Christians will basically agree with this criticism, in part or whole. But, they will insist, there are "some good ones." For example? *God's Not Dead*. There are now, I think, three films in the *God's Not Dead* cinematic universe, with new ones popping up every spring like weeds. The original, starring Kevin Sorbo, came out in 2014. I recently decided to sit down and give the film a chance.

It was much, much worse than I had ever imagined—possibly the most torturous thing any Christian has constructed since the Inquisition.

There are some perfectly decent Christian movies. *The Passion of the Christ* is great. But *God's Not Dead* does not come anywhere close to that category. It's not just bad because it's hokey and poorly written, though it is both of those things, but in a much more malignant sense. Like so much "Christian" fare these days, it insults its audience's intelligence, demonizes the outside world with cult propaganda, forgoes authenticity for emotional manipulation, and does it all under a slick, Jesus-y veneer. *God's Not Dead* perfectly encapsulates everything that is wrong with the Christian entertainment industry. For this reason, it's worth examining in greater depth.

Before I summarize the plot, such as it is, let me begin with a disclaimer: I will not bother naming any of the characters in the film. I won't bother giving them names because the filmmakers didn't bother giving them personalities. They are all caricatures: there's the Earnest Christian Student, the Grumpy Atheist Professor, the Ditzy Secular Girlfriend, the Bratty Liberal Blogger, the Wise Pastor, the Self-Absorbed Atheist Lawyer, the Fundamentalist Muslim Father, the Studious Chinese Student, and so forth. We also get cameo appearances from the Cool Black Guy, who—I swear I'm not making this up—introduces himself as "G-Dog," and the Slacker Classmate in a Baseball Cap, who, when warned by the professor that the course will be difficult, actually says, "Pffft, I'm out of here," and walks out of the room. They didn't show the part where he skateboards down to the local park and spray paints "Skool Sux" on the half-pipe, but we can fill in those blanks on our own.

Every atheist in the film is selfish and miserable. Every Christian is generous and wonderful. There are no shades in these sketches. At one point, the Self-Absorbed Atheist Lawyer is informed by his Bratty Liberal Blogger girlfriend that she has cancer. He blames her for ruining his day and dumps her on the spot. This was one of the film's subtler scenes.

The story revolves around the struggle between Earnest Christian Student (ECS) and Grumpy Atheist Professor (GAP). On the first day of philosophy class, GAP requires all students to write the phrase "God is dead" on a sheet of paper and sign it. They are supposed to do this, GAP explains, because religion is super lame. Of course, every kid in the class dutifully follows GAP's instructions—except for Earnest Christian Student. GAP warns ECS that if he will not sign this bizarre pledge, he will be required to present an argument proving God exists or else risk failing the class. Earnest Christian Student is a bit taken aback but accepts the challenge earnestly.

After research, prayer, and a pep talk from Wise Pastor, ECS comes up with three arguments to vindicate theism, which he presents in three separate segments dispersed throughout the film, in between scenes of a Muslim father abusing his daughter, atheists sipping cocktails and laughing at evangelicals, and other material lifted straight from your Aunt Marcy's email forwards. ECS argues, first, that God exists because the universe had a beginning. Second, that God exists because of the diversity of life and the suddenness with which it came into existence. Third, that God exists because without God there are no moral absolutes.

The first two arguments, as given, are among the weakest in the theistic arsenal, yet Grumpy Atheist Professor is flummoxed by them. He has no rebuttal except to quote the Book of Job and confess that he's only an atheist because his mom died of cancer. When ECS brings up the moral argument, GAP is again left stammering and fuming, as if it was the first time that he, *a philosophy professor*, has ever encountered the moral argument for the existence of God. The filmmakers may as well have included a scene where Richard Dawkins is left in stupefied silence because a creationist mentions the Cambrian explosion.

Finally, ECS wins the argument and the day by shouting, "Why do you hate God?" at GAP until GAP admits that, yes, he knows God exists, but he hates Him for killing his mother. The rest of the students in the class, who just weeks ago were prepared to swear to atheism, are converted to Christianity en masse. A few scenes later, Grumpy Atheist Professor is struck by a car on his way to a Christian rock concert and accepts Jesus as his Lord and Savior with his dying breath. Like I said, the bit with the atheist yelling at his girlfriend for getting cancer is nuanced compared to much of the rest of the film.

The way this movie tells it, the atheist case against the existence of God is entirely bereft of logic. This is a pleasant fantasy, but the problem is that most viewers don't realize it's a fantasy. They are being set up for a serious crisis of faith the moment they stumble across a Christopher Hitchens video or Bertrand Russell book. Grumpy Atheist Professor even allows Earnest Christian Student to sidestep the problem of suffering by gesturing to free will—without forcing him to explain how free will accounts for cancer and earthquakes. In real life, of course, no atheist will let you escape the challenge quite that easily. As a Christian, I believe it is a challenge that can be competently met, but *God's Not Dead* doesn't prepare you to meet it. The film only prepares you to engage with the sort of atheist who also happens to be a serial killer with an IQ of 45.

In another scene, Bratty Liberal Blogger (pre–cancer diagnosis) confronts one of the guys from *Duck Dynasty*, who randomly shows up because of course someone from *Duck Dynasty* has to show up in this type of movie. Bratty Liberal Blogger says she's offended that he "prays to Jesus openly." I was expecting her to then shout, "I'm a special snowflake" and run into a bunker marked "safe space," but I guess some things would be a little too obvious even for this movie. Now, a liberal might indeed confront someone from *Duck Dynasty* and harangue him about his faith—that part is plenty believable—but she will structure her complaint around the alleged "homophobia" of fundamentalist Christians like himself. That is not the route this fictional atheist takes, because every atheist in this movie always presents the weakest and most stereotypical version of the atheist argument and does so in the stupidest conceivable way.

So, what is the point of this movie or any like it? It's not a good primer for Christian apologetics because it avoids all of the intellectual and theological challenges for which a Christian might need to be primed. Sure, if an atheist ever argues his case by shouting "Stephen Hawking" over and over again before storming out of the room in tears (an actual scene from the film, almost), then you'll be equipped for the confrontation. But, then again, you don't need to be equipped for contrived arguments with perfect morons.

What else could it be trying to achieve? It certainly won't help you understand the other side, because in this film the other side is exclusively populated by psychotic, brain-damaged narcissists. In *The Brothers Karamazov*, Dostoevsky, a devout Christian, portrays his atheist foil as a brilliant, layered, tragic figure who articulates some of the most compelling arguments against theism that you will ever read anywhere. The folks behind *God's Not Dead* don't have the wit, courage, or integrity to challenge themselves and their audience in that way.

What's the point, then? *God's Not Dead* definitely won't help you better understand the difficulties of living as a Christian in the modern world, because in the film there are no difficulties. Every Christian is happy, satisfied, smart, attractive, well spoken, and supremely confident in his faith at all times. As far as I can tell, this movie exists first to turn a profit and second to give Christians cheap, empty pleasure. You are meant to walk out of the movie not with wisdom or understanding or knowledge or information or edification or enrichment, but with the cynical, hollow self-satisfaction that can be achieved only by building a gigantic straw man and burning it to ashes.

The Prosperity Gospel

Theologically, this all takes on its most dangerous form under the guise of the so-called "Prosperity Gospel." Snake-oil preachers have made themselves obscenely wealthy by preaching a Christianity of profit and material reward. Creflo Dollar, false teacher and founder of World Changers Church International, made headlines a few years ago when he somehow convinced his congregants to buy him a $65-million private jet. According to Dollar, his fancy aircraft and his opulent mansion are signs of God's love. As he has explained, "As the righteousness of God, your inheritance of wealth and riches is included in the 'spiritual blessings' (or spiritual things) the apostle Paul spoke of in Ephesians 1:5. Based on Psalm 112:3, righteousness, wealth and riches go hand-in-hand. You have every right to possess material wealth—clothes, jewelry, houses, cars and money—in abundance. It is that wealth that not only meets your needs, but also spreads the Gospel message and meets the needs of others."[2]

Of course, it's true that we have "every right" to possess wealth. It's also true that wealth is not in itself evil. But Christ makes it clear in Matthew 19:24 that wealth is more a burden than a blessing: "It is easier for a camel to go through the eye of a needle than for someone who is rich to enter the kingdom of God." The Epistle of James (5:1–3) makes the point in more dramatic terms: "Now listen, you rich people, weep and wail because of the misery that is coming on you. Your wealth has rotted, and moths have eaten your clothes. Your gold and silver are corroded. Their corrosion will testify against you and eat your flesh like fire. You have hoarded wealth in the last days."

The only mitigating fact about Creflo Dollar is that he lacks the subtlety and intelligence to effectively disguise the self-worship at the core of his teaching. If you go to Creflo Dollar to hear about the gospel, you know what you're going to get. Joel Osteen, the most famous Prosperity Gospel preacher on earth, is a bit cleverer in his approach. If you stumble across one of his sermons on television and happen to sit and watch it for a few minutes, you may not hear anything very objectionable at all. Sure, his style, the stage, the setting — all of it looks and sounds like ear-tickling televangelism. But you may have to listen closer and longer to actually hear the sacrilege come through.

In his book *Your Best Life Now*, a self-help manual masquerading as a spiritual devotional, Osteen gets right to heart of his theology: "We have to conceive it on the inside before we're ever going to receive it on the outside. If you don't think you can have something good, then you never will. . . . You must rid yourself of that small-minded thinking and start expecting God's blessings, start anticipating promotion and supernatural increase. You must conceive it in your heart before you can receive it."[3]

The essence of Osteen's message—and Dollar's and T. D. Jakes's and Paula White's and Jim Bakker's (before he went to prison for fraud)—is twofold: First, spiritual and temporal blessings flow not from God but from your own optimistic mind-set. You, the self, the individual, are the wellspring from which all good fortune flows. Think positive and positive results will inevitably follow.

Second, you must serve God and others so that you will in turn be served. A recent survey found that a third of American Christians believe that God will give you more money if you first give money to Him through tithing. God is like the stock market, according to this way of thinking: if you invest a small amount in Him today, He'll make you a millionaire tomorrow. And Creflo Dollar is the broker who can help to facilitate this transaction.

Where did these Christians get this idea? Well, from guys like Osteen. He said this in the same book mentioned above: "If you are generous to people in their time of need, God will make sure that other people are generous to you in your time of need."[4]

Osteen's version of generosity is inherently selfish. You are "generous" only because you expect to benefit from equal or greater generosity down the road. Osteen is not only leading his flock into moral and theological error but also setting them up for profound disappointment. The sad reality of life is that generous people are often taken advantage of, exploited, and then ignored when they hit hard times themselves. In fact, your generosity is not at all guaranteed to "pay off," ever, in this life. Jesus knew this, which is why He says in Luke 6:29, "If someone takes your coat, do not withhold your shirt from them."

He doesn't say, Give your cloak so that later on someone will compensate you for your loss by giving you an even nicer tunic. Instead He says, Give your cloak and be ready to give up the tunic, too, because there will always be someone coming and asking for more. It's not that we are supposed to allow ourselves to be fleeced and exploited, but that we cannot and should not expect to be reimbursed for our good deeds. We are to accept this reality, embrace it, because our lives are not about gaining earthly wealth and privilege. Our lives are not really about ourselves at all.

The Prosperity Gospel heretics spread the opposite message. Osteen's wife, Victoria Osteen, once put the case very directly: "When you come to church, when you worship Him, you're not doing it for

God really. You're doing it for yourself, because that's what makes God happy. Amen?"⁵

"Amen," shouts the Devil.

A Secular Religion

Secular society preaches its own Positivity or Prosperity Gospel. Indeed, secular society invented this gospel; it is the religion of secular people. Christians adopted it and tried to spiritualize it, but it remains a product of, by, and for secularism. Generations of children have been raised on "self-esteem" and "the power of positive thinking." An entire self-help industry has risen up to promulgate the idea that we can and should will ourselves into happiness.

This notion of self-willed happiness is ingrained in us from a young age. We are told by advertisements, by the media, by our schools, by Hollywood—by everyone—that we are wonderful and special and we should never for a moment allow ourselves to lapse into honest introspection or self-criticism. "You are enough!" "Live your truth!" "Love yourself!" "Embrace your flaws!" "You're perfect just the way you are!" These are the mantras of modern society and the modern church.

But it's useless. Try as we might, we can't actually convince ourselves to be always happy and always satisfied with ourselves. Indeed, the harder we try to muster those feelings, the more we focus on them and obsess over them, the more miserable we become. As much as we may heed the words of Osteen and Dollar and Tony Robbins, we find that our efforts to "name it and claim it"—to conjure good fortune out of the ether simply by thinking about it—ultimately fail. Let's examine why that might be the case.

The Agony of Being

There are many problems with these self-help mantras and the general attitude of positivity and optimism so deeply instilled in us. I would like to focus on only three. First, as I said, it is useless to insist that we must always be happy about life. Nobody ever has been, ever will be, or ever can be always happy. Life is not always a happy affair. Frequently it is unhappy. Sometimes it is a torment.

Life is painful. It can even be unbearable. This is a truth that the Bible does not attempt to hide. There is a whole book of the Old Testament devoted to it. And it is a truth that Christians have, until recent times, understood, embraced, and expressed with eloquence. Frederick W. Robertson once said, "You are tried alone; alone you pass into the desert; alone you are sifted by the world." Henry Ward Beecher added, "In this world, full often, our joys are only the tender shadows which our sorrows cast." These statements are profound and self-evident. We know that life is full of sorrows, we know that it feels very much like passing through a desert, because we have all lived life. There is no sense in denying its essence.

People suffer greatly in this world. We cannot hide from that reality and we should not shout clichés at it. The optimistic Christian slogans are a thousand times more irritating and damaging than the optimistic secular slogans. I would prefer to hear "If you can dream it, you can do it" a thousand more times if it meant I never again had to hear some well-meaning but obtuse Christian, often in the least appropriate situation, utter with oblivious confidence, "God will never give you more than you can handle!"

Who are we trying to fool? We certainly are not fooling the people who have, in fact, been given more than they can handle. There are some burdens so excruciating, so crushing, that there is no "handling" them. How do you "handle" it if your spouse abandons you?

How do you "handle" sexual abuse? How do you "handle" it when your child dies of cancer? You don't. You can't seize hold of these things and control them. They can't be "handled." They can only be suffered through. Anyone who has encountered the worst that life can throw at a person knows that you will not feel at all like you are handling it. You will feel like it is handling you. The best you can do is endure it, tread through it while you gasp and gurgle and struggle just to breathe. And there are some who fail to endure, even gaspingly. Suicide is a real problem in our society and becoming a greater problem by the year. Must we not admit that these people, at least, were given more than they could handle?

God will always give grace and strength to those who ask for it, and even to those who don't ask for it. But our slogans of positivity promise more than grace and strength. They promise that life will never come along and utterly flatten you. They promise that life will never give you a lasting pain. They promise that life will never overwhelm you. But it might do exactly that. It has done that to many millions of people. And we should not tell those people to "think positive" or "see the bright side," nor should we insist that they can "handle it." All they can do, and all we should urge them to do, is fall prostrate before God, abandoning themselves and their miseries to Him.

There is also a certain agony which springs not from any particular event or circumstance, but from the very fact of being. "To live is to suffer," says Nietzsche. He was wrong about many things, but not that. As Christians, we know that man is fallen. We know that he is separated from God. This is what gives us—or used to give us—our keen awareness of, and insight into, the pain of human existence.

It is a deeply terrifying thing to be conscious beings, able to contemplate our own mortality, and yet unable to do anything to prevent our inevitable demise. In his book *The End of Faith*, Sam Harris compares the human condition to that of a man who is told by his doctor that he has contracted a fatal virus that will surely kill him eventually, no matter what he does to treat the illness. As Harris points out, we are all born with that terminal diagnosis. But Harris is an atheist, so he has no consolation to offer for this unfortunate fact. In his view, we can only confront and accept it.

The picture is not so bleak for Christians, but it is still difficult in its way. It is a lonely thing to be, so far as we know, the only such beings in the physical universe, reaching always out beyond ourselves to a God we cannot see or touch or hear. The world tells us that the reason we cannot see or touch or hear God is that there is no God. If that were the case, then the life of a human being would be the cruelest joke nature has ever played. It would mean that she brings us into this world of misery, gives us the capacity to fully experience that misery, and then sends us hurtling back into eternal nothingness. It is no wonder that the worldly person is always trying to convince himself to be positive. If he ever stops whispering those mantras to himself, if he permits himself to contemplate the implications of his own belief system for a moment, he will come face-to-face with a yawning abyss that looms always over his head and will one day consume him. The optimism of an atheist is like the optimism of a heroin addict overdosing in the gutter. It is a momentary pleasure meant to mask a hopeless despair.

In *The Brothers Karamazov*, Dostoevsky wrote, "If you were to destroy in mankind the belief in immortality, not only love but every living force maintaining the life of the world would at once be dried up. Moreover, nothing then would be immoral, everything would be permissible, even cannibalism."[6] All of the Russian author's great works revolve, in one way or another, around this idea: that a life without God is not worth living—and barely livable. He is right. And it is better for the unbeliever to confront the spiritual desolation of unbelief, and to really feel its emptiness and coldness, than for him to push those thoughts away while still remaining in his squalid state. We are told that despair—or depression, as we call it today—is a mental illness. But how can we call someone ill for being in despair when he has so many good reasons for that despair? That's like seeing a man shivering and blue-lipped without a jacket in the freezing cold and advising him that his tremors must be a sign of Parkinson's. No, there is nothing wrong with his shivers. They are his body's way of telling him that he needs to go inside and get warm before hypothermia sets in. We do nothing for the man by treating his trembling while leaving him to die in the cold. We do nothing for a despairing man by numbing his sadness while leaving him to his empty, miserable existence.

There is no use telling a godless person to enjoy life. Kierkegaard said, "Listen to the cry of a woman in labor at the hour of giving birth—look at the dying man's struggle at his last extremity, and then tell me whether something that begins and ends thus could be intended for enjoyment."[7] If there is nothing beyond this life, and no greater purpose behind it, then he is right. Life moves always on to death. Every step we take is a step closer to it. If death is a plunge into nothingness, if it is the cessation of all being, then what is there but despair?

Imagine you are on a very long train with thousands of train cars in front of you. Now imagine that this train is careening off of a bridge, with one car at a time going over the edge. Perhaps you have a few minutes, a few hours—maybe, if the train is absurdly long, a few days. But your fate is set. You are going over. The train is not going anywhere but down. That is your destination. That is what life is like without God. Demanding positivity from the godless is like turning to the passenger in the seat next to you on that doomed train and saying, "Let's just enjoy the ride." Enjoyment would be impossible for a rational person in that situation. The only thing that would heal the despair would be news that the train is not falling over a bridge and into its own destruction—but instead transitioning to a new track entirely.

So what about those of us who know there is a God, who realize that the train is transitioning rather than crashing? Should we always be happy and positive? Certainly we should always have hope, but we must also have pain. The pain comes from our separation from God, and the knowledge of that separation, and the consciousness of our sin. There is no way to deny our separation and sinfulness, so the only thing a person can do with these facts, if he wishes to always be positive and optimistic, is get himself to the dangerous point where they no longer bother him. A Christian cannot but admit that God is remote from him. And he cannot but admit that he is a sinner, guilty of spiritual high crimes and misdemeanors. These truths should not make him perpetually gloomy, but confronting them means feeling a certain sorrow. Even the sweetest moments will have a tinge of bitterness—not a hopeless or resentful bitterness, but more like the bittersweetness of longing.

In his stunning work *Till We Have Faces*, C. S. Lewis captures this bittersweet longing: "The sweetest thing in all my life has been the longing—to reach the Mountain, to find the place where all the beauty came from—my country, the place where I ought to have been born. Do you think it all meant nothing, all the longing? The longing for home? For indeed it now feels not like going, but like going back."[8]

A few months ago I traveled to a city on the Pacific coast to speak at a fundraising banquet. That evening, after the banquet had concluded, I took a walk down to the beach and watched the sunset over the ocean. I felt refreshed and happy, but incomplete. I wished that I had my family with me. The sweetness of the moment was tinged with the bitterness of separation. I was happy, but my happiness was incomplete because I could not share the moment with those I loved. I think this is how the Christian ought to experience life. We can have happiness, but it will not be a full or perfect happiness until we are home with our Father. For now, we have the tender shadows. We can enjoy them—we should enjoy them—but not with the sort of enjoyment that banishes all pain and discomfort. For we cannot push away pain and discomfort without pushing away the God whose absence is their cause.

A Focus on Self

The other problem with the Positivity Gospel is that it turns my gaze back once again on myself. Religion becomes just another thing to make me feel better. Karl Marx famously called religion "the opiate of the people." Modern Christians seem to have taken that as a suggestion.

True Christianity is not at all like a drug. To authentically come to Christ is to become sober. It is to wake up to the truth, to see things for what they are, and to comprehend the very meaning and purpose of life. A Christian should be the greatest realist, because he knows reality and what lies behind it. He sees the forest and the trees and he knows about the roots beneath them and the force that gives life to everything. Most important, he is taken out of himself, away from himself, and into something greater and truer.

But the Christianity of false happiness and hollow positivity has the opposite effect. It obscures reality and brings us back into ourselves. It is the religion of Joyce Meyer, who infamously proclaimed, "I am not poor, I am not miserable and I am not a sinner."[9] Meyer may want to take another look at Luke 5:32: "I have not come to call the righteous but sinners to repentance." If she will not identify herself as a sinner, then she cannot identify herself as one called by Christ.

This is the fact we must accept: Jesus Christ did not traverse eternity, enter into our world, and accept a torturous death on the cross all so that we might feel better about ourselves. He came so that we might "have life and have it to the full" (John 10:10). Abundance does not refer to material possessions, for He tells us to renounce those. And life does not mean primarily our earthly existence, for He tells us that we must be willing to give that up. He came to lift us into the abundance of His Divinity, which is an abundance we can only accept and enjoy if we are willing to look beyond ourselves and let go of the wickedness and selfishness that closes us off from Him. This will not always be a pleasurable process, but it is a necessary one. After all, Christ only ever gave us one self-help tip. It was the very first thing He said when His public ministry began: "Repent and believe."

Christianity without the Cross

Here we arrive literally at the crux of the issue: the cross. The follower of the Positivity Gospel wants a Christianity without the cross. He cannot look to the cross and dwell upon it for very long because it is uncomfortable for him; it brings to mind arduous things like sorrow and sacrifice. If he glances at the cross at all, he doesn't see an instrument of unspeakable torture, which Our Lord in His victorious humility accepted and seized and then used as the ultimate weapon for good. Instead he sees a "Get Out of Hell Free" card. He concludes that Jesus died not to free him from sin but to free him to sin.

The unwise and irreverent Christian thinks that Jesus "paid the price for his sin" the same way his friend might pay for his bar tab on his birthday. That is what the cross becomes: an unlimited tab. A blank check. An eternal excuse.

No, it is none of those. It is horror, triumph, and destiny. It is horror because upon it the Son of God was brutally murdered, and in His incomprehensible agony He suffered the pains of every sin that ever was committed or ever would be committed. It is triumph because by the cross He conquered death and slew the dragon of sin. And it is destiny because Christ says, "Pick up your cross and follow me."

We will not escape our own suffering. Just because Christ paid the price for our sin does not mean that we pay no price. Salvation is free because there is nothing we can do to pay for it. We are infinitely valuable yet desperately poor. We cannot afford ourselves. But it does not follow that we are entitled to be free from all sacrifice, all pain, all difficulty, and all obligation.

We are invited into joy—a joy next to which modern positivity is a shriveled little thing. But in the cross we learn something about the nature of that joy. It is not a joy found by avoiding suffering. It is a joy found through suffering. Joy lies on the other side of a raging river of hardship. If we try to walk around the river, we will be walking forever parallel to joy, but always separated from it. If we busy ourselves with constructing a man-made bridge so that we can cross the river and keep our clothes dry—a bridge made of optimism and happy slogans and self-help jargon, as flimsy as cardboard—we will never make it across.

All we can do is plunge right in: swimming, trudging, staggering through the rapids, tripping over logs, slipping on the rocks, always against the current, always with great effort, always half submerged. We can have happiness even as we wade across, but that happiness comes from our knowledge that we are heading in the right direction, and from the moments of calm, where the current dies down and the water warms. And in those moments, we must resist the temptation to become complacent, stop swimming, and allow the current to carry us away. God gives us the calm so that we can move toward Him on the other side of the river, not so that we can drift further away.

If we really have faith and totally abandon ourselves to Christ, perhaps we will sometimes even be able to walk upon the water. But only a perfect faith can walk on water forever. Peter did not have such a faith, and neither do I. So I must embrace the struggle and learn to swim.

CHAPTER SIX

Diabolical Vanishing Act

Be alert and of sober mind. Your enemy the devil prowls around like a roaring lion looking for someone to devour.

—*1 Peter 5:8*

T his chapter is a necessary corollary to the previous one. I do not want to spend an exorbitant amount of time discussing the Devil, as I agree with C. S. Lewis that it is an error to feel an excessive and unhealthy interest in demons. I hope this chapter is not excessive or unhealthy. But I also agree with Lewis that the other error we can make, an equal and opposite one, is to disbelieve in demons entirely.[1] It is this error, and not the former, that most Christians in America seem to be making. This error is key in putting us on the wide road to destruction, because it tells us that there is no destruction. That is certainly a most attractive delusion, and perhaps the easiest to fall into, because the person we are disbelieving wants us to disbelieve him. It is difficult to ignore someone if he is are sitting in the room next to you and does not want to be ignored. It is not difficult if he is hiding under the bed.

A 2009 survey found that a majority of Christians believe—"strongly" or at least "somewhat"—that Satan is "not a living being but a symbol of evil." Another 8 percent don't know what they believe. Almost 10 percent only disagree "somewhat" with the idea that Satan is not real. That leaves just a quarter of American Christians who, according to this poll, totally accept the biblical teaching on this subject.[2] It seems that most Christians would tend to side with Episcopal priest Barbara Brown Taylor, who, in a 2014 interview with Religion News Service, said that the Devil is merely a "force for death." On the question of his literal existence, the prominent minister and theologian is agnostic.[3] United Church of Christ pastor Paul Lance recently informed his flock that the Devil is a "superstition."[4]

But the United Church of Christ is nothing more than a heresy factory these days, so it probably isn't fair to hold that pastor up as an example. Indeed, most priests and pastors of other denominations will not be as direct in their denial of Satan's existence. It is, rather, an implicit denial. A denial by omission. Whether or not they personally believe in some sort of Devil, they largely refrain from discussing him in their sermons. And whether their congregations answer "yes" or "no" when some survey-taker asks about this evil spirit, most of them think and live as though the Devil of scripture is nothing but a symbolic illustration or a kind of fictional mascot. For them, Satan is to evil what Tony the Tiger is to Frosted Flakes.

Satan in the Bible

In truth he is much more than that. Scripture is unambiguous about the reality of Satan, his aims, and his fate. We first meet Satan in the Garden of Eden (Genesis 3:1) precipitating the Fall of all mankind by tempting Eve to defy God. In Saint Augustine's view, the first reference to demons comes even before the serpent in the Garden.

He argued that the angels must have been made on the first day of Creation when God created the light, "saw that it was good" and "separated [it] from the darkness." Given that this occurs before the formation of the sun and all the stars, Augustine took this to be the light of goodness, which was divided from the darkness of evil after Satan and his legions rebel.[5]

Ezekiel tells us of an "anointed guardian cherub" who was made good and "blameless," but became "unrighteous." In Ezekiel 28:16, God says to Satan, "So I cast you as a profane thing from the mountain of God, and I destroyed you, O guardian cherub, from the midst of the stones of fire." Job 4:18 refers to this same event: "Behold He put no trust in His servant; and His angels He charged with folly."[6]

The New Testament is full of clear—and often terrifying—references to a personal demonic being who commands an army of evil spirits. It is no surprise that the powers of Hell should have come into greater focus when Our Lord was walking on the earth in physical form. As God burst into our realm, so did the forces of evil to meet Him.

St. Paul underscores the point with urgency: "For our struggle is not against flesh and blood, but against the rulers, against the authorities, against the powers of this dark world and against the spiritual forces of evil in the heavenly realms. Therefore put on the full armor of God, so that when the day of evil comes, you may be able to stand your ground, and after you have done everything, to stand" (Ephesians 6:12-13). St. Peter says that the angels who "sinned" were put in "chains of darkness to be held for judgment" (2 Peter 2:4).

We should not take the demons' "chains" to mean that they are confined to one corner of the universe, where they can do us no harm. The Bible is clear that Satan is active in our world. The "gloomy darkness" *is* this world, of which, according to Christ, Satan is the "ruler" (John 12:31). In fact, Christ interacts with Satan and his minions throughout the gospel accounts. He is shown driving out demons at various points, most notably in Mark 5:1–13, a passage that deserves to be quoted in full:

> They went across the lake to the region of the Gerasenes. When Jesus got out of the boat, a man with an impure spirit came from the tombs to meet him. This man lived in the tombs, and no one could bind him anymore, not even with a chain. For he had often been chained hand and foot, but he tore the chains apart and broke the irons on his feet. No one was strong enough to subdue him. Night and day among the tombs and in the hills he would cry out and cut himself with stones.
>
> When he saw Jesus from a distance, he ran and fell on his knees in front of him. He shouted at the top of his voice, "What do you want with me, Jesus, Son of the Most High God? In God's name don't torture me!" For Jesus had said to him, "Come out of this man, you impure spirit!"
>
> Then Jesus asked him, "What is your name?"
>
> "My name is Legion," he replied, "for we are many." And he begged Jesus again and again not to send them out of the area.
>
> A large herd of pigs was feeding on the nearby hillside. The demons begged Jesus, "Send us among the pigs; allow us to go into them." He gave them permission, and the impure spirits came out and went into the pigs. The herd, about two thousand in number, rushed down the steep bank into the lake and were drowned.

Here we learn that demons can enter into a human body, that they are numerous, and that thousands may occupy one body at a time. We also get a glimpse of the horror of Hell: these demonic creatures would rather be cast into a herd of swine than be sent back to the fires of eternal torment. It is a disturbing and confounding passage, yet it pales in comparison to Satan's first appearance in the New Testament.

Lessons from the Temptation of Christ

We are told that before He began His public ministry, Jesus retreated for forty days into the desert, days where he encountered Satan. Luke 4:3–13 describes the episode this way:

> The devil said to him, "If you are the Son of God, tell this stone to become bread."
>
> Jesus answered, "It is written: 'Man shall not live on bread alone.'"
>
> The devil led him up to a high place and showed him in an instant all the kingdoms of the world. And he said to him, "I will give you all their authority and splendor; it has been given to me, and I can give it to anyone I want to. If you worship me, it will all be yours."
>
> Jesus answered, "It is written: 'Worship the Lord your God and serve him only.'"
>
> The devil led him to Jerusalem and had him stand on the highest point of the temple. "If you are the Son of God," he said, "throw yourself down from here. For it is written:
>
> 'He will command his angels concerning you
>   to guard you carefully;
>   they will lift you up in their hands,
>   so that you will not strike your foot against a stone.'"
>
> Jesus answered, "It is said: 'Do not put the Lord your God to the test.'"

> When the devil had finished all this tempting, he left
> him until an opportune time.

It is important to note how Luke begins his account of the temptation. He says that Christ "was led" to the desert by the Holy Spirit
"to be tempted by the Devil." We are meant to understand that Jesus
was not caught off guard by any of this. It was no sneak attack by
Satan—at least not a successful ambush. Our Lord went out there to
meet him and engage with him. And He did actually engage. He
could have swatted the Devil away like a fly. He could have denied
the Evil One permission to approach Him in the first place. Instead,
He talks to him. He seems almost to humor him.

I think there must be at least two reasons for this: First, Jesus was
wholly human and wholly divine. To be human, He had to drink fully
from the cup of human experience. And there is no experience more
human than temptation. Second, I think it was strategic. Jesus
revealed and exposed Satan to us. He drew the snake out from under
the rock so that we could learn something about him and how he
operates.

What did we learn? Well, we learned foremost that the Devil is
real. He does exist. He is operating in this world. Jesus leaves us no
room to be mistaken about the situation. He is almost shouting to us
from the pages of scripture, saying, "Look, you fools! Wake up! Here
he is, doing his dastardly work." I have heard some people speculate
that Christ's temptation was an internal, not external, event. In this
view Satan is just a personification of Christ's mental and spiritual
struggle against His own dark urges. But Christ had no dark urges.
We who are merely human experience temptation internally because
we are fallen and corrupted. There are little cracks in our soul through
which evil can enter and do its work inside of us. Dostoevsky wrote
that the battlefield where God and the devil fight is the heart of man.[7]

Indeed, my heart is a battlefield, where my lower nature constantly wars against my higher nature. God guides me one way, but Satan entices me to go the opposite direction.

Yet the Sacred Heart of Jesus is not a place where the Devil can operate. Christ has no flaws for the Enemy to use as a foothold. He is uncorrupted and unfallen. Satan tempted Christ externally because that was his only option. You and I may feel enticed within ourselves to commit evil so that, for us, "temptation" means "the desire to do evil." Jesus, though, cannot be enticed to evil. He can have no desire to sin. Sin can only work on Christ from the outside, and then only so far as He permits. And Christ permitted sin to do quite a number on Him. He permitted it to nail Him to the cross. But sin never touched His heart. It never defiled Him from within, as it has done to me and to you. So Christ's temptation can only be read exactly as it is written. Satan, a real creature, approached Jesus Christ and, in his insatiable pride, tried to tempt the Son of God.

Next, we learn about the categories of temptation that Satan will use against us. Satan tempted Christ to turn stones into bread, appealing to appetite. Then Satan tempted Christ to worship him, the Devil, in exchange for all of the wealth and power in the world, appealing to the desire for wealth and power. Then, appealing to pride, Satan tempted Christ to fling Himself off a precipice so that the angels would come and rescue Him, thus demonstrating His magnificence and glory to the masses. It seems that Satan seeks to make us gluttons, materialists, or egoists. He will settle for just one, but often he has no problem convincing us to be all three.

Next, we learn how to handle these salvos from the Devil. Christ responded to each temptation by quoting scripture. This, again, was for our benefit. Our Lord didn't need to get into a theological debate with Satan. He didn't need to provide the Devil with any exegetical justifications for His actions. But He, the Word, leans on the Word, because that is what we must do when the Devil comes knocking on our door. Jesus is warning us not to rely on our own understanding, our own will, or our own strength when the forces of darkness are scheming against us. All we can do or should do is cleave to God, His Word, and His Righteousness. The Devil cannot carry us away when we are hugging tightly to the Lord. He cannot claim us when we are huddled under the cross.

The Fruits of Evil

That is why it is important to acknowledge the reality of the Devil. It is not that Lucifer deserves any sort of respect or recognition. It is rather that he cannot be resisted unless he has been recognized. William Lane Craig says that the primary work of demons, their main activity from now until the end-times, is to "destroy the servants of God." Their second goal, according to Craig, is to blind unbelievers to the truth of the gospel.[8] But it is apparent that Satan likes to combine these tactics. The Prince of Darkness would prefer to have everyone in the dark. He has set off a giant smoke screen in our culture, obscuring our view of everything—especially of himself. It is hard enough to fight an enemy you cannot see. It is impossible to fight an enemy you don't think exists.

But even with all of Satan's efforts to remain undercover, still it seems counterintuitive that Christians in our day would deny his existence. There is, after all, so much evidence of that fact. G. K. Chesterton observed that original sin is one of the only empirically provable Christian doctrines. The existence of demonic spirits would seem to be another. Indeed, denying the Devil in modern society is like denying germs in a sick ward or wind in a hurricane. The thing itself may be invisible to our eyes, but we are surrounded by its effects. We cannot see its form, but we can see its fruits.

All you have to do is turn on the news or go online. The Devil is always in the headlines, though not by name. Every year brings new school shootings and other mass-casualty events. There is terrorism. There is oppression and persecution across the globe. There are unspeakable crimes against children, especially those committed by clergy.

The sex abuse scandal in the Catholic Church is a giant, blinking neon sign announcing to all the world: "The Devil Exists." It is simply not possible that men could be so evil on their own. An infamous grand jury report in 2017 detailed some of the alleged behavior of priests in Pennsylvania. The only word you can use to describe the content of that report is "demonic." In one alleged case, a boy was forced to stand naked, posing like Christ on the cross while priests took pictures and added them to a collection of child pornography that they produced and distributed on the campus of the church. These priests would mark boys who were being groomed for abuse by giving them gold crosses to wear.

In another case, a priest raped a young girl and arranged for her to get an abortion. His bishop heard about the situation and wrote a letter of condolence—to the priest.

In another case, a priest molested a boy over the course of two years, admitted to church officials that he had engaged in naked "horseplay" with the child, and yet was allowed to continue in ministry for seven more years.

In another case, a priest raped a little girl while he was visiting her in the hospital.

In another case, a priest forced a boy to give him oral sex and then washed the boy's mouth with holy water.

In another case, a priest molested a twelve-year-old boy and admitted his crime to a church official, but the diocese ruled that the abuse wouldn't "necessarily be a horrendous trauma" to the victim.[9]

Most cases of abuse in the church are probably not as horrific as the ones described above. But these sensational examples show us the truly diabolical nature of the crimes. You can see the Devil leaping from the pages when you read them. And it's not surprising that clergy would fall so deeply under demonic influence. I believe it was St. Athanasius who first said, "The floor of Hell is paved with the skulls of bishops." St. John Chrysostom is purported to have said, "The road to Hell is paved with the bones of priests and monks, and the skulls of bishops are the lamp posts that light the path."[10]

Religious leaders will attract special attention from Satan. If they are weak, he will topple them with ease. The higher on the ladder they have climbed, the farther they will fall. It takes an angel to make a demon, after all. That is another Christian doctrine that seems to be verified by experience. Christians believe that demons were made from the stuff of angels, and Lucifer, before his fall, was higher in the angelic hierarchy than any of them. The principle at work here is simple: terribly beautiful things become terribly ugly when corrupted. Men in positions of great power will either be heroes or villains, without much room in between. Men who climb the closest to God can end up being the farthest away if they are not careful.

Of course, there are many other examples of demonic evil in the world. For better or worse, our twenty-four-hour news cycle keeps us abreast of all of it. There was the married couple in California who tortured, abused, and starved their thirteen children.[11] There was the man in Georgia convicted of murder after purposefully leaving his toddler to die in a hot car.[12] There was the mother in Texas who was sentenced to forty years in jail for trying to sell her two-year-old daughter into sex slavery.[13] And on and on. These cases of the darkest and bleakest sorts of evil should bring Satan clearly into view. Who can look at such acts and doubt the influence of the demonic?

In one of the starkest cases in recent memory, in 2017 a man shot and killed fifty-eight people from his hotel room in Las Vegas. Police investigated the attack for eight months and never found a motive. It seems as though the man just up and decided to slaughter dozens of human beings one day, and so he did. But nothing is done without motive. The problem is that you can't find the motive for these kinds of things by looking on the surface. If you investigate the problem deeper down, closer to its root, you hear the phrase that Jeremiah accuses Israel of shouting to the Lord, which is the same phrase that tradition attributes to Lucifer when he rebelled against God: "I will not serve."

We cannot find a clear motive for the basest of evils because there is no motive outside of itself. It is evil for evil's sake. Satan goes down because God goes up. Satan swerves left because God swerves right. Satan seeks to be (though, because he lacks God's power, can never truly succeed in being) God's antithesis. He does what is bad because God does what is good. And those who are most firmly in his grasp will act most explicitly with the same diabolical logic.

Lower Things

Atheists will point to all of this evil and use it as evidence against God's existence. They will insist that no truly good or loving God would allow such things to happen. A good God, they say, would reach out His hand and stop evil in its tracks. They do not understand that God made us free and gave us the power to choose. Love, by its nature, requires the consent of the will. God can compel our obedience. But even He cannot force us to love Him. If there is going to be the possibility of love, if we are going to have the power and the choice to love, then there must also be the possibility of hate, and the power and the choice to hate. God can and does intervene in any moment that He chooses to prevent this or that bad thing from happening, but in order to prevent all bad things from happening—in order to rule evil out in principle—He would have to either wipe humanity from the face of the earth or convert us all into automatons. There would be no pain, no evil, no suffering. But there would be no love, either, and no joy.

But there is another point to be made about evil. Not only does it not disprove God, but in fact it proves Him. For one thing, without God as the objective source of goodness and the standard by which goodness is measured, there is no basis upon which to call anything good, and thus no basis to call anything evil. For another, it is not possible to explain evil as a purely biological phenomenon. If it were, we would see mass murder, terrorism, and cruelty for cruelty's sake among other biological beings on earth. If evil is an offshoot or deformity of evolution, there is no reason why it should affect only the human species. Yet when a lion kills, we do not say that he has murdered. And when a dog copulates with another dog, we do not call it rape. We do not accuse animals of evil because we recognize that they are just doing what they are programmed to do. They are being themselves and acting in a completely natural way. It is all a part of the cycle of life, we say.

But among human beings, the story is very different. We make actual choices. A man can weigh the good path against the bad path and choose which one to walk. A man, if he is good, can transcend his nature and stretch himself beyond the limits of mere compulsion or instinct. A man can have a strong urge to preserve his own life yet sacrifice it for the sake of love or patriotism. It does not make any sense that evolution would produce in a man the ability, and the willingness, to give up his very existence for something higher. The fact that he reaches for this higher thing would seem to be compelling evidence that something higher than the merely biological exists.

On the other end of the spectrum, a bad man sinks below his nature and operates according to something even baser than compulsion or instinct. He destroys, he hurts, he mocks, he torments, he kills—and all because he thinks that through these actions he can attain some sort of power or freedom. This is not at all like a lion killing a zebra because of its predatory instinct. This is a man choosing to become a monster for reasons that cannot be explained in biological terms. As the good man reaches for the higher thing, the bad man reaches for the lower thing. And just as the former provides evidence for the existence of a higher thing, so the latter provides evidence for the existence of a lower thing.

Explaining Evil Away

Now, we have our modern and secular ways of explaining all of the brutality that surrounds us. Any time an act of great cruelty makes the news, we all shake our heads and solemnly resolve to finally address the mythological "mental health crisis" in America. Evil, we have decided, is a sickness. A mental illness. But as we have so far been unable to locate the evil cortex of the human brain, we are left assuming that the mass murderer, the rapist, the child abuser, and the sadist must be suffering from some sort of neurological mishap. Perhaps it has something to do with chemicals or synapses or transmitters. Just as despair must be psychological, so must sin.

Christians should—though most do not—reject this explanation. That isn't to say that mental illness is nonexistent or that evil men do not often have psychological problems. It is to say simply that the root of the evil cannot be found within the physiology of a person. Evil begins in the soul as a suggestion or a temptation. A person must choose whether to take the suggestion or not, whether to act on the temptation or not, whether to resist and flee the Devil (James 4:7) or not. This is how the Devil works on us most of the time. He is a "schemer," as St. Paul says, and he is looking always for an opportunity to lead us into wickedness. And once we have followed him into that dark, he will keep guiding us deeper and deeper into it.

Satan's ultimate goal is to possess us like property in Hell. Sometimes he—or his minions—may come to possess us in a different but related sense while we're still on earth. We cannot make the mistake of believing that demonic possession was unique to biblical times. Even less can we assume that demonic possession in the Bible was really mental illness misdiagnosed. We would do better to consider the possibility that some cases of mental illness in modern society are really demonic possession misdiagnosed. Our Christian ancestors, if they arrived here in a time machine, would immediately guess that a guy who shoots up an elementary school must be under demonic influence. We, on the other hand, do not even consider it a viable possibility. I think the ancients had a clearer view of things—on this point and many others.

As Christians, we have only two options:

1. We can conclude that the apostles, the prophets, and Christ Himself were all a bunch of superstitious, hallucinating fools and liars. We can declare the Devil a myth, Hell a deranged fantasy, and all of the cases of demonic possession—both ancient and modern—falsehoods and fabrications. But if that is our opinion, then it makes no sense for us to continue calling ourselves Christians. The atheists would be right, in that case, and the entire thing would be just a collection of ancient fables told by ignorant savages who didn't understand that all human evil is really the result of mental illness.

2. We can accept that demons are real, they are legion, they are prowling through the world seeking to devour our souls, and our struggle truly is not against any earthly force but against the "spiritual forces of evil in the heavenly realms" (Ephesians 6:12). We can believe, and tremble at the thought, that actual supernatural beings are hovering around us and working around the clock to guide us away from the light and into destruction. We can feel helpless against these beings, who are stronger and smarter than we'll ever be, and we can cling ever closer to God, who is our protection against the armies of Hell. We can take this threat seriously, and stop laughing about it like idiots and children, and we can take our faith seriously, because our faith is the only weapon we have and the only one we need.

Padre Pio once said that the devils are so numerous that if they all took bodily form, they'd blot out the sun. This is a horrific thought. But the true Christian does not deny it just because it is scary. Instead he takes shelter in Christ, and he marches on.[14]

Those are the two choices that present themselves. Or we can settle on the comfortable and cowardly, irrational option that lies between the two. We can continue claiming Christianity, wearing it around like a fashion statement, while taking to heart only the bits and pieces of it that make us feel warm and snuggly inside. We can proclaim a Good that triumphed over a nonexistent Evil, a Christ who delivered us from the clutches of a make-believe Devil. We can make a mockery of our faith in front of the entire world and give a false sense of security to the very souls who are most in danger of eternal damnation.

Satan would be okay with option one, but he much prefers we choose this in-between route. If we do, we become agents of Hell on earth even as we deny the reality of Hell. We become dupes of Satan—his favorite Christians. And he hopes we never repent, so that he can make our acquaintance in the afterlife.

CHAPTER SEVEN

Strength in Numbers

Do not conform to the pattern of this world, but be transformed by the renewing of your mind.

—*Romans 12:2*

"The times they are a-changing," Bob Dylan sings.[1] And he's right. Time does change. Time is the agent of change. But the truth does not change along with the time, because the truth stands outside of time. What was good and holy two thousand years ago is good and holy now. What was debased and evil two thousand years ago is debased and evil now. Our ability or willingness to discern one from the other may have changed, but the reality has not.

We seem to be confused on this point. We think that the essence of reality—and especially of moral reality—has changed, for the better, over time. Our "chronological snobbery," as C. S. Lewis called it,[2] may be justified when it comes to technology and medicine, but it is disastrous in the area of theology and morality. It is one thing to prefer the new iPhone to the brick-sized mobile phone your dad carried around in his fanny pack in 1992; it is quite another to prefer newer notions of moral and theological truths to the moral and theological truths espoused by Christ and affirmed by the church for two millennia. But this is precisely what we have done. We have decided that our technological superiority must somehow ensure moral superiority, as if our high-tech gadgets have given us access to a higher understanding of life.

The modernist assault on the faith does not revolve around any one particular doctrine. Christians today, unless they are Jehovah's Witnesses, are not likely to outright deny the Trinity or Christ's humanity. Arianism and Docetism were heresies for a more thoughtful age. The heretics of the past at least had the wit and wherewithal to attack a specific dogma and suggest a different dogma to take its place. But modernism is, as Pope Pius X described it, an obscure "synthesis of heresies."[3] In practice, it is more of a general feeling or a prejudice. The modernist, moved by emotion and self-interest, cooks up an incoherent heretical stew whose ingredients can hardly be identified. He isn't so much worried about the theological points. He could take or leave the Trinity, the Resurrection, the Incarnation, and the atonement. His real beef is with Christian morality.

The Bible on the Back Burner

If there is any single doctrine that the modernist might bother denying, it would be biblical inerrancy—the belief that the Bible is divinely inspired and teaches the truth without error. Former megachurch pastor Rob Bell flatly rejected the Bible's divine inspiration in 2015 when he told Oprah that the church will make itself "irrelevant" if it continues to condemn gay marriage on the basis of "letters from 2,000 years ago."[4] In Bell's opinion, which is shared by many modernists, the Bible is a rather suspect collection of myths and editorials written by ignorant goatherds and fishermen who were blinded by contemporary prejudices. I once gave a talk on religious liberty at Catholic University and was informed by a student during the Q&A that Jesus Himself saw the world through a lens of first-century bigotry. A large majority of the students in attendance—some of whom were standing in the back of the room and solemnly holding a giant rainbow flag—seemed to agree.

But it would be a mistake to assume that modernism hinges entirely on the question of inerrancy. When influential evangelical Jen Hatmaker came out in favor of gay marriage a couple of years ago, she claimed that gay relationships can be holy.[5] To Hatmaker and many other modernists, sacred scripture is a faultless, error-free crossword puzzle whose deepest truths have lain hidden for centuries. On the other hand, Father James Martin, a prominent and far-left Catholic priest, didn't bother offering any biblical rationale at all when he urged Christians to celebrate "gay pride."[6] And the Protestant ministers who gather around abortion clinics to offer prayers of blessing and encouragement likewise do not pretend to do so on a scriptural basis.[7]

A similarly confused view is held by the many churches that have, over the past several decades, uncovered a biblical mandate to marry, divorce, and remarry an unlimited number of times. These churches will allow one man to stand in front of the congregation and marry a succession of different women, while pretending to fully accept the inerrancy of Christ's prohibition of divorce and remarriage (Matthew 5:32). The modernist is simply interested in affirming his own lifestyle, choices, and priorities. If he has to deny scripture to secure this permission, he will do so. If he's clever enough to mine the permission out of scripture, he will do that instead.

The New Awareness

Surveys show that 75 percent of American Christians believe the Bible is the Word of God.[8] That leaves only 25 percent who claim that the Bible is fallible. Interestingly, however, more than 25 percent of Catholics, mainline Protestants, and evangelical Protestants favor gay marriage. More than 25 percent in every group believe that abortion should be legal in all or most cases.[9] Significantly more than 25 percent in every group believe that the marital union is not necessarily permanent or inseparable.[10] Yet the Bible—the "Word of God," according to three quarters of American Christians—explicitly forbids the homosexual act (1 Corinthians 6:9–11), the murder of human beings (Exodus 20:13), and divorce (Luke 16:18). How can so many Christians profess to believe in the inerrancy of scripture while simultaneously maintaining positions that oppose scripture?

There is a fair amount of biblical ignorance at play here. But, even more to the point, most of these Christians have never made any attempt to harmonize their moral views with the Bible. These modernists have a nebulous sense that there has been some sort of awakening in recent times and now the hardest commands and edicts in the Bible have evolved or dissolved, or that newer and more enlightened truths have finally risen to the surface after centuries buried under the muck of ancient bigotries.

Pope Francis helpfully summarized the position in 2018 when he declared capital punishment "inadmissible," insisting that modern society has recently discovered the evils of the death penalty, in our new moral "awareness."[11] He offered no rational or theological explanation as to how a thing that God not only permitted but expressly commanded (Genesis 9:6) could be "inadmissible." There is no rational or theological explanation to give. Modernism is not a rational or theological phenomenon. Modernism is a feeling—the feeling that the most popular opinion, the most comfortable, the most modern, the most convenient, must be correct.

The Most Unpopular Position

I have already mentioned homosexuality and gay marriage. I should probably dwell on it for a few moments because this is probably the issue, more than any other, where even faithful Christians wish to find some sort of harmony between the Christian view and the worldly view. Unfortunately, no such harmony is possible. To adopt any part of the world's view on the question of homosexual marriage or homosexual acts, you simply have to deny, implicitly or explicitly, the truth and authority of Christianity. A person cannot go to the moon without leaving earth, no matter how much he may wish to stand on earth and the moon at the same time. In the same way, a person cannot adopt the morality of modern society without leaving the Christian faith behind. The two stand in direct contradiction to one another. You must choose one or the other, or some third option in opposition to both.

At the moment I am not interested in discussing whether Christianity is right about homosexuality. That is beside the present point. The present point is simply that Christianity *does have* a teaching on the subject, and if you wish to remain Christian, you cannot disagree with that teaching. The Bible clearly and repeatedly condemns homosexual acts, including in 1 Corinthians 6:9–11, Romans 1:26–27, 1 Timothy 1:10, and all across the Old Testament, most notably in Leviticus 18:22 and Genesis 19:1–38. Moreover, Jesus Christ defines marriage. In both Matthew and Mark, He teaches that marriage is when a "man" and "his wife" come together and "become one flesh."

There is a full, uncompromising, explicit consensus across both the Old and New Testaments about the nature of marriage and the moral depravity of homosexual acts. Every Christian church affirmed these teachings for almost two thousand years, during which time no Christian theologian or thinker of any note found, or claimed to find, any pro-gay interpretation of the verses mentioned above. That is because no such interpretation can be found. We must either accept with humility the biblical teaching on this topic, or we must throw the Bible out—and Christianity with it.

If we try to retain both our gay-affirming views and our Christian faith, then we must do so on the basis of one of the following three principles:

1. The Bible is wrong about homosexuality.
2. Homosexuality was wrong during biblical times but is no longer wrong.
3. The Bible actually endorses homosexuality, but its approval is so subtle and hidden that nobody noticed it for twenty centuries until we came along and discovered it.

The first principle denies the moral authority of scripture. And if the Bible contains moral error—and such egregious error—then we have no reason to believe anything else it tells us. If we cannot believe what scripture tells us, then we have no reason to believe that our faith is true.

The second principle exchanges objective morality for moral relativism. And moral relativism is incompatible with Christianity because, in the Christian understanding, morality is grounded in, and flows from, an eternal, perfect, all-knowing, and changeless God. If morality is relative, then God is either imperfect and changeable— or nonexistent.

The third is no better than the other two. Leaving aside the strik-ing arrogance of such a view, it also supposes that the Bible is so confusing and incomprehensible that even its clearest commands and edicts cannot be known. In other words, the Bible may mean the opposite of what it says, and it may take a couple of millennia to real-ize it. So what opposite meanings will humanity discover in the year 4000? Perhaps it will turn out that the Bible's references to Jesus as "the Son of God" actually meant "not the Son of God." Anything is possible. And if anything is possible, then Christianity ceases to be intelligible or meaningful.

One of these claims, at least, is implicitly made every time a Christian preaches the holiness of homosexual acts. That is why we "conservative Christians" are so insistent in our rebuttals. It is not that we have some obsession with homosexuality, or that we hate gay people. We are simply defending the truth of our faith, which these "tolerant" Christians are directly attacking.

That is why I encourage Christians like Jen Hatmaker to drop the act and admit that they are not believing Christians. They do not believe that the Bible is a reliable source for moral truth. They do not believe in the Christian moral teachings that were unanimous across every church for almost two thousand years. They do not believe what the Gospels say about Christ's own words, or else they do not believe that Christ is an absolute moral authority. In other words, they have the same view of scripture, Christian teaching, and Jesus Christ that all non-Christians do. And they are free to hold that view. Billions of people across the world hold it. I think they are wrong for holding it, but I would never be angry at a non-Christian for being a non-Christian. I do, however, feel anger towards apostates and her-etics who lack the integrity to admit to themselves and the world that they are apostates and heretics.

Christianity would be greatly benefited if those who have already implicitly disavowed the faith would now make their disavowal explicit and public. The world would be benefited, too, because then it would have a clearer understanding of what Christianity is and what it isn't. And the apostates and heretics themselves would benefit because then they would be forced to finally confront their position—and it is only in such a confrontation that repentance can occur.

The Pull of the Crowd

A lot of this boils down to peer pressure. We may not really agree with the popular ideas and philosophies of the day, but we don't want to be on the outside looking in. No matter how often we were told as children not to follow the crowd, still the crowd has a significant gravitational pull. In the 1950s, psychologist Solomon Asch conducted an experiment to test the strength of that gravitational pull. He showed his subjects two cards. One card had one line, and the other card had three lines of varying lengths. The subject was asked which of the three lines on the second card matched the length of the line on the first. The answer was intentionally obvious. But there was a catch: the participants were tested in groups of eight, and all of the members of each group, save one, were actors. Asch wanted to find out whether the real subject would give a clearly wrong answer if the actors gave the wrong answer first. In the end, 75 percent of the real participants conformed to the crowd by giving the wrong answer at least once. Only 25 percent were entirely unswayed by peer pressure.[12]

A real-life version of this experiment has been unfolding before our eyes. For the majority of human history, it was taken for granted that a person's status as "man" or "woman" was purely biological and determined by his or her sex at birth. Nobody had any notion of a "gender spectrum" or "gender fluidity." There have always been effeminate men and masculine women, but there was never any thought given to the possibility that the effeminate man might really be a woman, and the masculine woman might really be a man. But as the irrational, anti-scientific, and superstitious belief in "transgenderism" was introduced into the cultural bloodstream by academia and Hollywood, individual Americans, feeling the increasing peer pressure, quickly forsook their knowledge of basic human biology and adopted progressive gender theory wholesale. Now, roughly half of all Americans believe that a man can be a woman even if he was born with a penis. Even among the oldest Americans, nearly 40 percent believe that a person's gender might be different from his or her biological sex.[13]

The numbers aren't much better among Christians. Thirty-five percent of Protestants and 46 percent of Catholics now believe that a person's sex might be different from his or her sex at birth.[14] These Christians apparently have not read even the first chapter of their own Holy Book, which declares unambiguously that "male and female He created them" (Genesis 1:27). What would the results of these surveys have been if they had been conducted fifty years ago? A hundred years ago? Five hundred years ago? Well, we don't know for sure because nobody ever thought to ask the question. The answer was utterly self-evident to everyone. Now we deny the self-evident because everyone else denies it. The church is a "reed swaying in the wind," and the wind is blowing fiercely and confusedly in one direction, then another.

Our culture has many ways of forcing this particular delusion upon us, especially through the manipulation of language. We are told that people may come up with their own "preferred pronouns" and it is then our obligation to use them when referring to those persons. This is nonsense, of course. You don't get your own "preferred pronouns" for the same reason that you don't get your own "preferred prepositions." These aren't subjective terms. These are classes of words that exist to convey factual information, not feelings.

You can't stand on a platform and then require everyone to affirm that you are standing off the platform because "off" is your favorite preposition. It doesn't matter what preposition you prefer. You're either on or off the platform, and what I say about your relationship to the platform will depend entirely on the actual physical reality of the situation, not how you feel about that reality. My primary responsibility when talking to someone else or to you is to convey the truth. That is quite literally the entire point of verbal interaction. That's why lies are such terrible things, because they deprive the people who hear them of something they are owed—the truth—and because they sow confusion and undermine our ability to communicate with one another.

If I say you're standing off a platform when you're actually standing on it, I've told a lie. Even if I told the lie to make you feel better, I have still lied, and lying is bad. That's why I don't want to lie, and you cannot force me to lie on your behalf. You can lie to yourself all you want, but you cannot drag me into it. And so it goes for pronouns. If I intentionally call a man "she," I have lied. I have conveyed something that isn't true. Despite my polite intentions, all I've done is contribute to the confusion, dishonesty, and intellectual chaos rampant in our culture.

Words have meanings. If you were to search for the word "he" in the dictionary, you would find that it is, by definition, a pronoun used to refer to a male human being or animal. If you're a male human or animal, that's your pronoun. Or, I should say, that's the pronoun that applies to you. You don't own it. You can't change it or reject it or outlaw it any more than you can change, reject, or outlaw gravity. It is what it is, you are what you are, and words mean what they mean. Your feelings do not come into play here at all. They have absolutely no bearing whatsoever on the meanings of things.

Of course, there is a third option when it comes to pronouns. New ones have been invented—made-up pronouns like "ze" and "xu"—for people who do not feel that their essence is fully captured by either set of available options. But if I call a man a ze or a xu or a zir or a wu or a ca or a cat in the hat or wocket in my pocket, I have skipped right over lying and descended into utter nonsense. That I have done it at someone else's behest doesn't make it any less nonsensical. It's like seeing a crazy man on the street shouting at a stop sign and running up to participate in the argument. The man isn't less crazy just because you've plunged down the rabbit hole of insanity with him. The stop sign won't suddenly start talking now that two people are trying to coax some words out of it. The reality is still the reality.

Here's what it comes down to: I am not morally or ethically required to speak nonsense or tell lies for anyone's sake. On the contrary, my moral duty is to do exactly the opposite. I'm supposed to tell the truth, regardless of how the truth makes anyone feel. That is what both scripture and common sense dictate.

The Big Deal

I think the influence of the crowd may tempt us into two other, subtler errors. First, in a world so drenched in sin, we may develop the general impression that sin must not be that big a deal. Indeed, North Raleigh Community Church, pastored by an apostate pastor named John Pavlovitz, makes this declaration explicitly on its website. "We believe sin is not that big a deal," it says. Most of us would not be so up-front about this belief, but it is something we harbor in the back of our minds. Everyone is out there sinning. Sin is totally normal, totally casual, totally a part of everyday life. It can't be all that bad, can it?

There are a few sins that we do consider to be "big deals." They are the ones that the civil authorities recognize as serious, the ones that can land you in jail, the ones that most people never do and are never tempted to do. It is likely that you have never personally known a murderer, a rapist, an arsonist, or an armed robber. It is even more likely that you have never committed those sins or felt the slightest inclination to commit them. Those sins are faceless and nameless and alien to you. Yes, of course they are bad. It is easy to see the badness, and it costs you nothing to call it out.

But everyone tells lies. Everyone gossips. Everyone commits petty acts of cruelty. Lots of people look at pornography. Lots of people have sex outside of marriage. Lots of people use the Lord's name in vain. How could these things be so bad if they are so commonplace? How could they be so bad if your friendly neighbor Jim, who always invites you to his backyard barbecues and even let you borrow his garden hose last week, has done them? How could they be so bad if your best friend and your spouse and your mother have all done them? Most of all, how could they be so bad if *you* have done them? You are decent and ordinary and hardworking. You pay your taxes and recycle. You make friendly small talk on elevators. You are likable and charming. You return your shopping cart to its proper receptacle. So you watch inappropriate things on the internet sometimes. So you tell a lie here and there. So you enjoy a juicy bit of gossip on occasion. Who doesn't? You're entitled to these minor lapses, aren't you? Everyone carries on this way, after all. What's the big deal?

We even have a certain sense that there must be strength in numbers. Again, this is a mostly ambiguous sense and never something we would say out loud, but it is there. We think that if everyone is committing the same sorts of sins and being evil in the same sorts of ways, then surely God will have to adjust His standards a bit. If we present a united front come Judgment Day, we can force Him to the bargaining table. What else is He going to do? He can't damn us all, we think. That would be like an employer firing his entire workforce because they've gone on strike to demand more vacation time and better benefits.

We are mistaken. We will all be judged alone, just as we are born alone, just as we die alone. We will not be considered as a collective or graded on a curve according to the standards of the day. There is only one objective standard—God's. And that is the one He will apply to us.

Before we take comfort in the thought that our sins might get lost in the shuffle, or that they aren't a big deal because everyone else does the same, we must remember that Christ came to die for each of us individually. He did not die for sin as an abstraction. He died for your sins, specifically, and for mine. Even our little sins cannot be so little if they nailed the Son of God to the cross. And the sheer quantity of sin throughout the world and through history does not, to any degree whatsoever, lessen the severity of a single sin individually. Christ suffered many lashes at the pillar. That does not excuse or mitigate the one that I delivered.

We might think of it this way. If your spouse cheats on you, the betrayal will not be easier to endure just because so many other people have had to endure similar betrayals by their own spouses. A man cannot admit to an affair with his secretary and then soften the blow by assuring his wife that many other men have had affairs with their secretaries. His point is true but irrelevant. If anything, the prevalence of the sin may only worsen the impact. His wife already knew that there are many lying, lecherous men in the world, but she thought her husband was different from those others. He certainly pretended to be different and had an obligation to be different. Now all she can do is look at him and say, like Julius Caesar, "Et tu?" I imagine that God looks at us, in our betrayals and spiritual adulteries, and says the same. Et tu?

A Low Bar

I think there is another similar error that the crowd may indirectly lead us into. It is even harder to detect within ourselves. Even if we basically concede that sin is a terrible thing, and even if we generally agree that evil does not become less evil when it becomes more frequent, we may imagine that the bar for virtue has been lowered. In a world where goodness is so scarce, we may think it is quite sufficient if we have the faintest hint of virtue, or make the feeblest attempt at a good deed, or fulfill our most basic obligations. I know that I am tempted strongly in this direction.

Just the other day I skipped my evening prayers because I didn't want to turn the TV off. I justified the decision to myself by pointing out that I had gone to church that morning. Most people don't bother to go to church. Most people don't bother to pray. I thought that I must be ahead of the game because I had gone to church and I did at least consider praying. I had made it over the bar. Not the bar God sets, but the bar society sets. I was like a guy who leaves the house looking like an unkempt slob but feels proud of himself because most of the people he passes on the street look slobbier than he does—and anyway, at least he combed his hair.

This calculation sounds ridiculous and arrogant when I write it down like this. That's why I normally refrain from writing it down or saying it aloud or thinking it consciously. It is mostly just a cloudy, impalpable feeling that I carry around with me. If I give a certain amount to charity, I know that it is not as much as I could give, but at least it is more than what most people give. If I lend a helping hand to someone, I know that I could have done more, but at least I did something. If I exhibit any modesty or charity or generosity, I know that it was only a meager amount, but at least I made the attempt. I am always trying to exceed the standards of the world by just a hair's breadth. Just enough, I think. I am shooting for the bare minimum.

God does not want my bare minimum. God does not want me to go just one step further than other people. He does not say, "Be good enough." He does not say, "Be better than most." He says, "Be perfect." Of course, it's hard to shoot for perfection. It is all the harder when you are surrounded by people who are not even trying. The world tells us that there is no such thing as good or bad. All is permissible. Sin is no big deal. Some sins are even laudatory. There is no perfection. But Christ calls us out of that relativistic fog—all the way out. Not to mere acceptability or decency, but to holiness, to sainthood. He will settle for nothing less, so neither can we.

CHAPTER EIGHT

The False Virtues

For this very reason, make every effort to add to your
faith goodness; and to goodness, knowledge.

—2 Peter 1:5

I t is easy to be virtuous in our world because we have adopted easy virtues. We applaud ourselves for our goodness, but it costs nothing to be "good" in modern times. A man can be good just by sitting in his living room. The couch potato is the new paragon of virtue, exceeded in goodness only by the man in a coma. Virtue has been pulled down from its lofty perch and made accessible to the inert. By this standard, the most virtuous thing on the planet is a turnip or a blade of grass. It just sits there and says nothing and does nothing and does not get in the way.

The church, once the stalwart defender of real virtues, now promotes cheap and shallow ones. Christians are not often exhorted to courage, chastity, fidelity, temperance, and modesty anymore. Those virtues require action and sacrifice and intention and thought and sometimes pain. They ask you to do something for their sake,

become something, be something. These are the formidable, inconvenient virtues. You must rise to them because they will not come
down to you.

Luckily for us, we are no longer asked to strive for those high
virtues. Instead we are encouraged to be welcoming, accepting, and
tolerant. The turnip virtues. Compassionate, too. Always compassionate. And I agree, of course, that a Christian ought to be welcoming, accepting, and tolerant. Certainly he must be compassionate.
But these virtues have superseded and ultimately consumed all the
others.

Welcoming

"All are welcome, all are welcome, all are welcome in this place,"
goes the nauseous hymn popular in Catholic churches throughout
my childhood.[1] This indeed has been the motto of most churches
across most branches and denominations for the better part of a
century. All are welcome. Throw open the doors and let everyone in.

I do not disagree with the sentiment, as far as it goes. But it
doesn't, or shouldn't, go nearly as far as we tend to take it. Yes, we
should welcome everyone; the questions are *what* we are welcoming
them into, and *why* we are welcoming them into it. The answer to the
first question is obvious enough: the church, the truth, Christ. Why?
Repentance, joy, completion, eternal life. "Let the children come to
me, and do not hinder them," Christ says (Matthew 19:14). Come *to
me*, though. Not nearby, or close enough, or to some general approx-
imation of me. Come to me, with all that means and entails.

It is significant, I think, that the "come to me" verse is sand-
wiched in between two of Christ's hardest teachings. In the immediately preceding verse, Our Lord gives His teaching on divorce,
forbidding it in most cases and equating remarriage with adultery

(Matthew 19:4–9). Right after "come to me"—"just then," according to Matthew—He tells the rich young man to give all of his possessions to the poor if he wishes to be perfect. Then Christ utters one of the most difficult lines in all of scripture: "Truly I tell you, it is hard for someone who is rich to enter the kingdom of heaven. Again I tell you, it is easier for a camel to go through the eye of a needle than for someone who is rich to enter the kingdom of God" (Matthew 19:23–24).

This all happens in the moments before and after Our Lord admonishes His disciples for preventing the little ones from approaching Him. It is rather conspicuous that "let them come" is quoted so often, while the verses surrounding it are usually ignored. But they cannot be ignored, because they give us an idea as to what coming to Him actually involves. Christ wished that all would come, He turned no one away, but He could not and would not stop them from turning themselves away. They had to make the choice to accept the truth or not. He knew that His teachings were impossible for human beings to follow on our own, so He invites us to take a leap and rely on God: "With man this is impossible, but with God all things are possible" (Matthew 19:26).

Christ's welcome is always within the context of Truth, with full disclosure and respect for the free will of the individual. Christ will not compromise with you, nor will He compel you. He says: *Here I am, here is the Truth, here is what you must do and how you must live. Please come to me, and have life in abundance.* The "welcome" of the church and of every Christian should follow this same model. We bring the Truth to the world and welcome everyone to accept it and live by it. We cannot welcome them to the Truth by forfeiting or hiding the Truth. We cannot "bury the lede," as it were, and try to get people into the church on some other grounds, with plans to spring the Truth on them later when they're already committed.

And yet that is what "welcoming" in a modern church context often means. We try to entice the world into the church by fashioning the church to look and sound exactly like the world. In the end, we are welcoming the world back into itself. We are welcoming it to remain exactly where it is, doing exactly what it was already doing. We are not inviting the homeless into our home so that he can get warm. We are rather tearing down our own walls and inviting the homeless man to freeze alongside us. He is just as cold as he was before, and nobody is better off.

When a large evangelical church in Colorado set out to become more "welcoming" recently, it decided that including open homosexuals in every level of leadership and ministry was the best way to achieve that goal. The pastor also invited church ministers to "follow their hearts" on the question of officiating at gay weddings. This sort of welcome is increasingly common in churches around the country, and to what end? You have only welcomed the world into the same unbiblical, relativistic view it had already long since adopted and proclaimed. Indeed, you have not welcomed the world at all. The world has welcomed you.

Acceptance and Tolerance

I will fold acceptance and tolerance together here because they are generally treated as if interchangeable. In modern parlance they're both just extensions of "welcoming." To welcome is to tolerate, to tolerate is to accept. This is wrong, of course. It is possible to be welcoming toward someone without necessarily tolerating his behavior, and it is possible to tolerate someone without accepting everything he does. Our culture demands acceptance—more than that, celebration—of all lifestyles and life choices, but it often makes those demands under the guise of less intrusive sounding words like "tolerance" and "welcoming."

In a literal sense, to tolerate something is merely to allow it to exist. If this is all that the champions of tolerance are asking of us, then they are not really asking anything. Every person I refrain from killing or kidnapping, I have tolerated. Since I have not killed or kidnapped anyone, I have successfully tolerated everyone on the planet. I am perfectly tolerant. I am even tolerant of all ideas and beliefs and opinions, because I have not taken any steps to forcibly eradicate them. I have argued against them, encouraged others to adopt different views, but I have always done it tolerantly; that is, I have always done it while allowing everyone to ultimately decide for themselves. By this standard, nearly everyone on the planet who is not a murderer, a dictator, or an Islamic militant is tolerant. It is the lowest bar in the world, the easiest to get over. You don't even need to jump. Which is probably why the Bible never mentions the word "tolerance," except to warn that Judgment Day will not be "tolerable" for unrepentant sinners (Luke 10:14). Tolerance is never given as its own commandment because it's sufficiently covered by the commandment against murder.

But as we've established, people don't really mean tolerance when they advocate tolerance. It is not enough for you to simply allow for the existence of sinful people and behaviors. You must accept them. Accept, dictionary definition: to receive willingly, to give approval to, to endure without protest, to regard as proper, to make a favorable response to. Synonyms: accede, assent, concede, acquiesce, capitulate. It is quite possible to tolerate without accepting, which is why accepting is the point, not tolerating. The church, according to the culture, must do much more than tolerate our sins. It must accept—acquiesce to, assent to—those sins.

Once again, the Bible has nothing at all to say in support of this notion. The word "acceptance" is never mentioned. The concept is addressed, but often to the opposite effect. St. Paul exhorts his readers to avoid even associating with, much less accepting, those who are profligate and public in their sin (1 Corinthians 5:11). In his letter to the Romans, St. Paul does tell us to "accept" the behavior of our brothers and sisters in faith—but only where it is morally neutral. "Do not quarrel over disputable matters," he says, such as what sort of food we're supposed to eat (Romans 14:1). As for sin, he urges us to put on the sacred armor of faith and prayer and war against the Devil, who is trying to trick us into sinning (Ephesians 6:11).

There are stories of true acceptance all throughout the Gospels, but never the sort of carte blanche, ask-nothing-of-me, progressive acceptance that we favor these days. Jesus accepts the Samaritan woman at the well (John 4), but the acceptance requires that the woman confront and acknowledge her sin. Jesus accepts the Canaanite woman and acquiesces to her request that He heal her daughter (Matthew 15:21), but the woman must first humble herself. The parable of the prodigal son is one of welcoming and acceptance, but the father only accepts the erring son once he repents of his ways and returns home. We cannot be truly accepted until we have abandoned those parts of ourselves that are fundamentally unacceptable. Acceptance, like reconciliation, is a two-way street.

There's a quote that has become a well-traveled internet meme, often (and, I think, wrongly) attributed to Marilyn Monroe. It usually goes like this: "If you can't accept me at my worst, you don't deserve me at my best." Sometimes it says "handle" instead of "accept," but the meaning is the same. It's no wonder that the divorce rate is so high in a society where this sort of tripe passes for relationship wisdom. You are destined to be alone and miserable forever if you go around insisting that your friends and loved ones only "deserve" you if they are willing to "accept" the worst parts about you—as if enduring your most selfish and objectionable behavior is the price of admission. I think (or hope, anyway) that most people aren't quite so obnoxious as to proudly and explicitly adopt this motto. But it's a popular meme for a reason. Whether they would state it explicitly or not, many people do believe, deep down, that they have a right to total acceptance. That is, every part of themselves, all of their attitudes and inclinations and behaviors, should be accepted by their friends and loved ones and acquaintances, and especially by the church.

No. The bad parts of ourselves should not be accepted by anyone, least of all by the people who love us and who care about our spiritual well-being. This is why God will especially refuse to "accept us at our worst," and why His church ought to follow suit. The alternative to acceptance, in this case, is not a wholesale rejection. Rather, we are urged and besought and counseled to improve for our own sake, for the sake of growth, maturity, and joy. This is the message the church should send. Come one and all, it ought to say, come in your sin and your weakness and your brokenness. Come with all that is ugly and rotten about you. Come with all of the darkness within you. *Come and be healed*. Be changed. Be made something entirely different. No, this is not a message of acceptance. It is something so much greater than measly acceptance. It is a message of salvation.

Of course, what makes people feel most unaccepted and unwelcome in the church are the "rules." There are rules to Christianity, if you want to put it that way, but they are not arbitrary. Our Lord's exhortations and commandments are "rules" in the same way that gravity is a rule. It's not something randomly invented just to cramp our styles. It is something intrinsic; something fundamental to reality itself.

When St. Paul says that "neither the sexually immoral nor idolaters nor adulterers nor men who have sex with men nor thieves nor the greedy nor drunkards nor slanderers nor swindlers will inherit the kingdom of God" (1 Corinthians 6:9–10), he is informing us of a fact of life and of the afterlife. Such people, if they are unrepentant, cannot enter the Kingdom. It's not simply that God won't let them, as if He decided this but just as easily could have decided otherwise. The point is that a person who has structured his life around sin, and for whom sin is life's primary joy, cannot exist in Heaven. As C. S. Lewis has observed, he wouldn't enjoy it anyway.[2] The only joy of Heaven is in worshiping God, and a person who has never learned to find joy in that, and has never tried to learn, cannot be a part of the heavenly community. Putting such a soul in Heaven would be like digging some worm-like creature from deep underground and expecting it to live on the surface of the earth, basking in the rays of the sun. The very sun that gives us life would cook such a creature alive and destroy it. It has adapted itself to living in the dirt and cannot live any other way. I will have more to say about this at the end of the book.

Judgment

Wrapped up in all of this talk of acceptance and tolerance is the matter of judgment. The worst thing in the world, we are told, is to judge. We must never judge, never be judgmental. We are constantly reminded that Jesus said, "Do not judge" (Matthew 7:1). And those three words have become the most popular words ever uttered by Our Lord. We like to pretend that everything else He said is summarized by this one phrase. We treat "Do not judge" as the distillation of His life and ministry. There are over seven hundred thousand words in the Bible (yes, I counted), and we have come to believe that they all can be condensed down into those three. We're wrong.

Yes, He does tell us not to judge. But to understand what "Do not judge" actually means, and how it ought to apply to our lives, we have to look at those words in the context of Christ's teachings. We don't even have to look very hard, because He makes the point clear in the very same chapter of the Bible. Here is the full verse from the seventh chapter of Matthew:

> Do not judge, or you too will be judged. For in the same way you judge others, you will be judged, and with the measure you use, it will be measured to you. Why do you look at the speck of sawdust in your brother's eye and pay no attention to the plank in your own eye? How can you say to your brother, "Let me take the speck out of your eye," when all the time there is a plank in your own eye? You hypocrite, first take the plank out of your own eye, and then you will see clearly to remove the speck from your brother's eye.

The point here is that we must judge rightly and fairly, as Jesus says specifically in John 7:24: "Stop judging by mere appearances, but instead judge correctly." The whole Bible is chock-full of judgments we are told to make about ourselves, about others, about actions and things and situations. Of course Jesus is not warning against judgment per se. He is warning, instead, against hypocritical and self-serving judgments. He says we must attend to the plank in our own eyes rather than focusing on the dust in our brother's eye. But He does not recommend that we just leave our brother there to deal with the dust on his own. He tells us to take the plank out of our own eyes first and then help with the dust. This is both a practical and moral prescription. Moral because ignoring your plank would be self-righteous and dishonest. Practical because you cannot see well enough to handle the dust problem if you've got a big plank sticking in your eye.

Judgment is good. We are commanded to judge. But our judgments themselves must be good, and made out of love and concern for our brother.

Compassion

This brings us finally to compassion. Our culture loves compassion, or at least its version of compassion. But it means the same thing by compassion as it means by tolerance and acceptance. All of these terms have been squished together and then wrung dry. We have turned many different and diverse words into bland redundancies. The poverty of language in modern society is a problem unto itself, and not one I have the space to expand upon.

So when Christians are urged to be "compassionate," we know what is really meant: Shut up and go with the flow. Mind your business. Don't make people feel bad about their choices. This is not only *not* compassionate; it is, in fact, the exact opposite of compassionate. True compassion is a strong and vibrant and heroic thing. Compassion comes from the Latin for "co-suffering." To be compassionate towards others is to take on their suffering, to share in their pain in the hopes of guiding them towards a good end. Christ showed us the most perfect form of compassion when He came and suffered and died for the sins of man. Christ's passion was compassion, co-suffering. He took on our pain and felt it for us.

But to suffer for our sins, He first had to see them and recognize them for the dirty, deadly things they are. To be compassionate to us amidst our sin He had to be unaccepting and intolerant of our sin. This is what compassion means. It is suffering. It is sacrifice. Compassion is not always polite. It is rarely easygoing. It is never enabling, never passive. Its aim, ultimately, is Heaven. That is the sort of compassion we receive from Him, and it is the sort of compassion we should give to others.

The faux compassion we are called to these days is just indifference by another name. The "compassionate" person of this sort really cares primarily about his own comfort. Helping others overcome sin and temptation would make him uncomfortable because it would force him to confront the darkness in his own soul, so he says nothing and does nothing, and he tells himself that his selfishness is love and his cowardice is courage. His compassion is a compassion entirely devoid of compassion. In fact, his compassion is a grave injustice. When he says we ought to "accept" all "lifestyles," however sinful, and that we ought never speak of Hell or call anything a sin, he is doing actual harm to his brothers and sisters in Christ. It's not just that he's failing to help them, but that he's actively hurting them. With this attitude and approach—this "compassion"—he does great damage to two groups of people.

First, he does damage to the habitual and unrepentant sinner whose sin is being so politely and nicely tolerated. It may be true that this person will feel relieved to be encouraged in his wickedness and told that it's really very good and natural for him to do whatever it is he wants to do. He may be grateful for such an assurance. For now. But the wickedness he partakes in is still destroying him all the same. He is brought closer to eternal damnation all the same. And for us to facilitate this easy and casual descent into the fires of Hell is not compassionate. It's rather like giving a man morphine so he no longer feels any pain from the cancer in his lungs. It is nice that he feels no pain, but the cancer is still eating him from the inside. Better that he feel the pain, at least for a time, so that he will go and seek treatment and be healed. In the same way, it is better that the sinner feel the weight of his sin and save his soul.

The second group of people deeply harmed by this fake "compassion" are those who wish to avoid sinning. This is perhaps the most neglected group in all of Western Christendom—those who are filthy sinners but who actually want to be holy and need some help and encouragement in that direction. It seems that the church has nothing at all to say to these folks, except that they're wasting their energy and should just relax and go with the flow.

As a member of this second group (and sometimes of the first), I can testify to the poisonous effects of our culture's permissive "compassion." I take it personally when these "compassionate" folks go around saying that there is no sin and everything is fine. I take it personally because I can look in my own soul and see this for the insidious, satanic lie that it is. I know I'm a sinner. I know I'm weak. I know I'm a coward. If left to my own devices, cut off from the grace of God, encouraged to indulge in my basest instincts, Lord only knows the evil I could commit.

The moral obligations of our faith are a great challenge for me, as I am such a frail and flimsy human being. I am always looking for an escape hatch. A way out. A rationalization. An excuse. "Well, this isn't so bad. I can do this. I can carry on this way. It's all right. Everyone's doing it." These are the words Satan whispers in my ear every hour of the day, and I wish sometimes that they were true.

The absolute worst thing you can do, then, is feed into or encourage my weakest and most selfish inclinations. The least compassionate response on your part is to agree with the devil on my shoulder. Now, in the moment I may love you for it—*Hooray! You told me what I want to hear! You made my life easier!*—but if I listen to you, if I really take your words to heart and convince myself that my sins are not sins, that my wickedness is not so wicked, then one day, I imagine, I'll be cursing your name forever in the pit of Hell. And perhaps, if you carry on with this "compassion" of yours, eventually I'll be able to do so in person.

The world is full of weak, pitiful sinners like myself, people just looking for a way around our duties and obligations. A way to follow Christ without taking up our cross. A way to be a Christian without making sacrifices. A way to enter Heaven while holding onto a piece of earth. How does your so-called compassion help us? How have you equipped and strengthened us in our spiritual battle by telling us that we need not battle? And how is this "compassion" any different from the "compassion" of the Devil?

The fight to be forthright, chaste, modest, courageous, and pure in this decadent and decaying culture is constant, exhausting, and often quite confusing. Those of us who even so much as desire, on some level, to be good, to be true—even if we are so incredibly terrible at following through—are already in a small minority. And so the most compassionate thing you can do for us is to say: *Yes, you're right to struggle. You're right to fight. You're right to resist Satan at any cost. You are not wasting your energies. And when you fail, you're right to crawl back to God on your hands and knees begging for mercy. You're right to do these things. Keep doing them. It is worth it in the end. Resist sin. Lean on God's understanding, not your own. Put on the whole armor of God. Beat back the Evil One with all you've got, scratching and clawing and gouging at his eyes. Keep going. What you fight against, this sin you struggle against, it is as horrible and disgusting as you believe it to be, and more so. Do not give into it. The fate of your soul hangs in the balance. You can't give up. Keep fighting. Let me help you. Let me fight with you. Let me suffer with you. Let me walk ahead of you and show you the way. Let me demonstrate the obedient Christian life for you. Let me be a light in the storm.*

This is what Christ has said to all of us, and our job as compassionate Christians is to echo His words and say to each other what He would say if He were standing physically in our midst. This is the truly compassionate message. Maybe it's not the easy version or the fashionable one or the one that makes for pithy slogans and Facebook memes, but this is how we ought to be encouraging, exhorting, and edifying each other. That is, if we actually love each other. If we actually want each other to go to Heaven. But if we're satisfied to have as much fun as possible now and pay the bill later in eternity, then by all means we ought to continue with that more tolerant and popular form of compassion. We will be walking to our own destruction, but at least we'll be comfortable until we get there.

True Compassion

How can we as mere mortals exhibit true, authentic, meaningful compassion that mirrors the compassion Christ showed for us? We will never have the opportunity to die on a literal cross for the sins of others. We cannot redeem even ourselves, much less the world, through our suffering. So how can we be compassionate like Him whose power and goodness far exceeds our grasp?

The author David Foster Wallace—not a professing Christian by any means—provides a pretty vivid image of earthly compassion in his "This Is Water" commencement speech, which he delivered at Kenyon College in 2005. After discussing the miserable, self-centered "default setting" most of us tend to operate on, he said this: "But if you really learn how to pay attention, then you will know there are other options. It will actually be within your power to experience a crowded, hot, slow, consumer-hell type situation as not only meaningful, but sacred, on fire with the same force that made the stars: love, fellowship, the mystical oneness of all things deep down."[3]

He doesn't connect the dots all the way to God, but the dots are clearly visible. The "force that made the stars" is the Divine Force, God. Compassion springs from the recognition of that holy force in others. We can be compassionate, and empathetic, once we confront the fundamental sacredness in all created beings. We are all truly "one," in the sense that we are bound together and held in existence by the Lord of All Things. "Truly I tell you, whatever you did for one of the least of these brothers and sisters of mine, you did for me," says Christ. He does not just create and then cast aside. He remains in His creation. He resides within each person. And if we look with eyes that see, if we pay attention, as Wallace recommends, we can see that cosmic spark, that supernatural fire, that gives us life and unites us.

This is where we find Christian compassion in its fullest and strongest form. It is a compassion that fans the divine flame. Compassion that ignores sin, or nods approvingly at it, is not compassion at all. It is not love. It may be tolerance and acceptance, but it tolerates and accepts the destruction and damnation of human life.

A Good Hatred

Before I bring this chapter to a close, I'd like to say a word about hatred. While our world proclaims easy virtues, it also condemns easy vices. Even the most limp-wristed and cowardly of pastors, the kind who will not denounce sin in any form, will still have no problem wagging his finger over the alleged evils of hatred. But hatred in and of itself is not evil. Hatred can in fact be a good thing, even a beautiful thing.

We should bear in mind that indifference, not hatred, is love's opposite. Hatred is a part of love and a sign of its vitality. Hatred is love in its ferocious and militant form. Whether it is a good hatred or a bad hatred depends on what, precisely, it is aimed at. Hatred aimed at the cancer patient is bad. Hatred aimed at the patient's cancer is good. Not just acceptable, or admissible, but *good*. If you love a person, you must hate his cancer. There is no way to love someone while being indifferent, or tolerant, toward the disease that ravages him.

Hatred always seeks to annihilate. So we should not want to rid the world of hatred unless we have rid it of all the things worth annihilating. Unfortunately, we have not accomplished that task and never will. There are many ugly, terrible, deadly, revolting things in our world, and we must have a raw, raging hatred for all of them—especially sin.

The Bible repeatedly speaks of this holy and righteous hatred, and commands us—not merely allows us, but commands us—to have this sort of hatred in our hearts:

- Psalm 97: "Let those who love the Lord hate evil."
- Proverbs 8:13: "To fear the Lord is to hate evil."
- Romans 12:9: "Hate what is evil, cling to what is good."
- Proverbs mentions seven things that God Himself hates, and in four places in the Bible (Genesis 4:10, Genesis 17:20, Exodus 2:23, James 5:4) we are told of sins so abominable that they "cry out" to Him for vengeance.

A passage in Revelation is particularly interesting: "I know your deeds, your hard work and your perseverance. I know that you cannot tolerate wicked people. . . . Yet I hold this against you: You have forsaken the love you had at first. Consider how far you have fallen! Repent and do the things you did at first. If you do not repent, I will come to you and remove your lampstand from its place. But you have this in your favor: You hate the practices of the Nicolaitans, which I also hate."

God can find few redeeming qualities in the church in Ephesus—except for its hatred and intolerance. Those are the two things He cites *positively*, the two that they need *not* repent of. What redeeming qualities will He find in the church in America? We have forsaken both love and hatred. We tolerate wicked people and have little hatred for even the most horrific practices. We seem to think that all of our other sins will be overlooked because at least we are so tolerant, but the opposite is the case. Our tolerance will not compensate for our other sins because our tolerance is one of our greatest sins.

Tolerance is never commanded or even mentioned in the Bible because it is a false virtue. A Christian should be too busy loving and hating to worry about tolerating anything. He should love God and his fellow man and all that is good and holy. He should hate sin, the Devil, and all that is disordered and unholy. He should only "tolerate" that which has no moral significance whatsoever. He should tolerate the color of his neighbor's car and the shape of his neighbor's head. But he should hate his neighbor's wickedness just as he should hate his own wickedness. And the more he loves God, the greater this hatred will be. If he cannot hate wickedness—if he cannot even conceive of hating it—then he is nowhere in the vicinity of loving God.

It will be cautioned that we must always make sure to love the sinner as we hate his sin. This is true, of course. But there usually isn't a conflict between those two things. We hate a sinner's sin *because* we love him and God. If we hate the sinner, then we probably won't have much urge to hate his sin. We will more likely take pleasure in his sin because it destroys the person we hate. When you really hate someone, you do not feel disappointment or sadness when you hear about the bad things they've done. Rather you are amused, even delighted. That's why people enjoy gossiping about those they dislike.

I think the temptation to hate the sin and the sinner together really only arises when the sin is so monstrous, and our revulsion so intense, that we have trouble separating the two. It is easy to hate white lies yet love the white liar. It is much more difficult to hate the child rape and love the child rapist. The latter sin is of a nature and to a degree that our faculties for reason break down and the militant side of love takes over. We want to destroy the sin and everything associated with it because it is so unthinkably grievous. The sinner has descended deep into the darkness and we can barely see him and his humanity down there. In our hatred, we want to toss a grenade into that hole and blow all that is inside it to bits—the sin, the sinner, everything.

We are wrong for this, and we should repent of it. But we should be worried if we do not experience this temptation at all. I suppose it could mean that we are saintly and enlightened. More likely, it means that we are indifferent. And there is nothing more dangerous for a Christian than that.

CHAPTER NINE

In and of the World

For what do righteousness and wickedness have in common? Or what fellowship can light have with darkness?

—*2 Corinthians 6:14*

T he 2018 Met Gala went Catholic. The Metropolitan Museum of Art's Costume Institute held its spring exhibit with the theme "Heavenly Bodies: Fashion and the Catholic Imagination." Many famous celebrities came to partake in the festivities, some of them dressed in sexualized clerical attire, some in risqué outfits with bedazzled halos around their heads, some as scantily clad angels. Rihanna wore a sexy pope costume. There was a bondage mask covered in rosaries. The attendees snacked on champagne-flavored crosses. It was exactly the sort of sacrilegious affair you would expect. Here's something else that, sadly, you might expect: the eminent Cardinal Timothy Dolan, archbishop of New York, attended the event. The cardinal wined and dined and rubbed elbows with the very people who had come there to mock him and desecrate his faith. Jesus would have overturned the tables. Cardinal Dolan sat down and ate at them.

I cite this incident not because it is an especially egregious example of cowardice among Christian "leaders." It is egregious, of course, but not especially so. Not by current standards. I cite it because it is emblematic, a perfect illustration of the church's relationship with the world in modern times: the relationship that a chameleon has with the branch he is sitting on. It blends in, disappears. Rather than being parts of the Body of Christ, as St. Paul describes us (1 Corinthians 12:27), we have become appendages of the world. One with it. Members of it. Indistinguishable from it.

Christian culture and secular culture cannot merge into one. It is a zero-sum game. Secular culture openly and aggressively militates against our faith and everything associated with it. It is intent on undermining and destroying Christian values. We cannot marry ourselves to it, we cannot join it, without forfeiting our Christian identity.

Screen-Obsessed

Americans spend about eleven hours a day consuming media in various forms. This would be a problem irrespective of faith, because it prevents us from living an authentic human existence and reduces us to the status of spectators. But the problem is exacerbated for Christians because much of the media we ingest is avowedly hostile to Christianity. If I tried to list all of the examples of anti-Christian bias in media, this book would balloon to the size of the Bible and it would still only tell half the story.

Here are just a few of the most obvious and explicit examples. The show *Lucifer*, which debuted on Fox in 2016 and now runs on Netflix, tells the story of the biblical Devil: a witty, decent, nice-looking fellow who abandoned Hell and came to earth to help solve crimes. There's also *Preacher* on AMC, based on the comic book about an alcoholic preacher who becomes possessed by the love child of an angel and a demon and then embarks on a mission to find God, Who has abdicated His heavenly throne. *Impastor* on TV Land is about a hard-core gambling addict who assumes the identity of a gay Lutheran pastor. All of these shows delight in sacrilege, and there are many others in the same vein.

The ABC show *Scandal* once aired an episode where the protagonist got an abortion while "Silent Night" played in the background.[1] This is the same network that produced a show called *Good Christian Bitches* a while back, so we shouldn't be surprised. The show didn't catch on, and neither did ABC's *The Real O'Neals*, a comedy about a Catholic family where one of the children is gay, the other is an atheist, and the parents are getting a divorce. The networks don't always find commercial success with their anti-Christian propaganda, but that doesn't stop them from trying.

And this is to say nothing of the *Family Guy* episode where Jesus has sex with a married woman,[2] or the episode of *Curb Your Enthusiasm* several years ago where Larry David pees on a picture of Christ.[3] As I said, there are many examples of Hollywood openly and gleefully mocking Christianity. But it's not the open and gleeful mocking that's really a problem. It's easy enough to avoid watching a show where Satan is a crime fighter. What's far more dangerous is the show or film that embeds nihilistic and hedonistic themes in a story line that never directly touches on anything religious or spiritual. And this describes the vast majority of the content churned out by Hollywood on a weekly basis. We Christians sit and absorb it into our minds and souls, rarely stopping to question the messages we are receiving.

We tell ourselves that all the time spent watching TV or binging Netflix is just an "escape," an opportunity to "turn our brains off" and "relax" for a while. The problem is that we are always escaping. Our brains spend most of the day in the "off" position. And in this submissive, malleable state, we are utterly susceptible to whatever ideas or messages Hollywood wants to feed us. Television is a passive experience, which makes it the perfect medium for shaping minds. The unresisting mind is most easily shaped. Especially an unresisting mind that does not realize it is being shaped. We begin to act like the people we see on TV, dress like them, speak like them, think like them; we adopt their viewpoints and priorities. We do all of this without noticing it. Five or six or seven hours a day watching TV, thirty-five or forty hours a week, two thousand hours a year, year after year—after a while, we cannot distinguish our real lives from the fantasy world we enter through the screen.

The same problem presents itself with the internet, which takes up at least half of our eleven hours of daily screen time. I make my living on the internet, and I have seen its pitfalls firsthand. Worse, I am what we call a "content creator." We "content creators" create content. Just content. Stuff for you to see or watch or read, consume in whatever way, and then promptly forget. You don't care about the content of the content, and most content creators don't care, either. The internet has become, mostly, a place for people to find content, and see content, and share content, all for content's sake. Think of how many hours of your life you have spent mindlessly scrolling a newsfeed. It is like you are searching desperately for some particular piece of content, some special thing, but really you are just looking for content of any form, content that will distract you for ten seconds, and then another piece of content for another ten seconds, and then another piece, and on and on. Many websites these days are built with something called "infinite scrolling"—an apt name. It means that you can keep scrolling down and new content will continuously load, forever, into infinity. I have often cringed in contemplating just how ridiculous I will feel on my deathbed for wasting so much time mind-lessly staring at my phone.

The average American spends twenty-five hours a week online, or thereabouts, in addition to his thirty-five or forty hours of TV a week. That's sixty hours, if you're keeping track. It's no wonder peo-ple don't read books or make home-cooked meals anymore. They don't have time. Almost every waking hour not spent in the office is spent staring at one screen or another. And of course the problem is worse for the younger age brackets. Teens basically never look up from their phones. We're going to be a nation of hunchbacks soon enough. Hunchbacks who can't remember anything or pay attention to anything or interact with other human beings in a real-life setting.

You can see the effects of this internet addiction everywhere, perhaps most notably in the decline of language. We went from scrawling hieroglyphics on the cave wall to scrawling hieroglyphics (emojis, as we call them) on the Facebook wall. It would appear that the average American, at this point, is unable to communicate emo-tion without using little pictures or short video clips to indicate whether he is happy or sad.

And this is to say nothing of all the pornography. Americans watch an enormous amount of internet porn. Just one porn website reported several billion hours of porn consumed across the world in one year. That adds up to five hundred thousand years of porn. In a decade, we will have viewed over five million years of porn. Consid-ering that the average age of first exposure to pornography is now ten, we can assume that children will account for a sizable portion of that five-million-year chunk.

Much could be written, and has been written, about the disas-trous effect all of this screen time has on our bodies, minds, and souls, but here is, I think, the worst effect of all: we have forfeited our interior lives. People often worry that we have replaced our social lives, our interpersonal existence, with the internet. This is true and concerning. But even more concerning is the death of intrapersonal existence. The internet is a place for people to spill out thoughts they otherwise would have, and should have, kept to themselves; to explore the weird and dark desires they otherwise would have, and should have, controlled and suppressed; to follow a half-formed train of thought they otherwise would have, and should have, taken more time to form completely. The internet is not just a meeting place, a communication system, a black hole of pictures and sounds, and a brothel—although it is all of those things. It is also our brain. It does our thinking for us. It quite literally completes our sentences. And this is why we like the internet so much. It keeps us stimulated and distracted, so that we never have to confront who we are, what sort of people we have become.

Despite what the show *God Friended Me* on CBS might imply, God does not speak to us directly through email or Twitter messages. He speaks to us internally, in our hearts, and often His voice is no louder than a whisper, easily muffled or ignored if we aren't paying attention. What this means is that we need to have a vibrant and active intrapersonal existence. We need to be "in touch with ourselves," as a therapist might put it. We need to have moments of silence and quiet and contemplation. Almost all of those moments, for us, are cannibalized by social media or Netflix or cable.

It's Just Entertainment

But many of us Christians have decided that our entertainment choices ought to be exempt from moral scrutiny. We've come to the convenient conclusion that television is a neutral medium. We need not even engage with someone who suggests that a certain TV show or movie is not helpful in our Christian walk. "It's just entertainment," we respond with a shrug. Which is a bit like saying "It's just food" when someone warns that a Cinnabon won't help us lose weight.

It's one thing for us to debate which shows or movies bring us closer to God. That's a healthy discussion. It's quite another for Christians to claim that we shouldn't even take such concerns into consideration. I'm willing to listen to an argument that a show I've written off as morally objectionable is actually edifying. But I have little patience for an argument that a show isn't morally objectionable because it's morally neutral. I could take more seriously the assertion that *The Walking Dead* is a spiritually enlightening masterpiece (it isn't) than an argument that watching a guy get his face eaten is an entirely neutral experience that leaves no mark on our souls at all.

Nothing you do is morally neutral. Your clothing, your diet, the way you speak, even the kinds of thoughts you allow yourself to think—none of these are neutral. They are for good or ill, one way or another. There certainly is no moral neutrality in the sorts of images and ideas you choose to spend several hours a day passively ingesting. You are either being hurt or helped by them. Most of the time, you're hurt.

We often pretend not to believe or understand this simple concept. When St. Paul said, "Whatever you do, do it all for the glory of God," we imagine that he meant to include a disclaimer, but somehow forgot: *Whatever you do—except for the thing that you spend the majority of your free time doing, and that influences human behavior to such an extent that companies spend billions of dollars advertising through it—*do it for the glory of God. Quite a boneheaded oversight on the great apostle's part. Or else a boneheaded interpretation on ours.

Here's a question: If TV is such a neutral thing, if it's "not a big deal," then why do we defend our TV-watching habits so passionately? Why do we consider it "unrealistic" to curtail those habits?

Because TV is not neutral. Entertainment is a force. It moves us. That's why we value it so highly. That's why we spend hours a day with it. That's why actors in this country make millions of dollars. We value what they do more than we value pretty much anything else. There is much to be said about that fact, but you cannot pretend it shows TV is morally insignificant.

The Benedict Option

In his book *The Benedict Option*, Rod Dreher argues that Christians need to put some distance between themselves and the world. It is not that we should flee into the mountains never to return (though I would be personally amenable to such an arrangement), but rather that we need to protect our Christian identity, and foster it in our children, and in order to do that, we must give ourselves some space.[4] Our faith begins to suffocate and die if we are constantly immersed in the world and its value system. Perhaps a "bubble," of sorts, is exactly what we need to construct for ourselves. Not a prison, or a cave, or a cage, but a spiritual buffer zone. This zone should be, if nowhere else, in our homes, where we can collect ourselves and convene with our families and our God. The problem is that screens scattered everywhere around the house, including in everyone's pockets, provide a portal through which the secular world and all of its vices can invade, plant its flag, and establish its dominion where it does not belong.

Christians today recoil at the idea that they should ever recoil from contact with the world. Such a suggestion will be met with familiar slogans: "We can't put ourselves in a bubble." "In the world, not of the world." "Don't put your light under a bushel." And so on. The Christian who does not want to forfeit any of his voluminous entertainment time will pretend that such a sacrifice would somehow interfere with his Christian witness.

Unsurprisingly, scripture does not endorse this view. Far from recommending that we always, all the time, be in contact with sin and darkness, it says exactly the opposite. In his first letter to the Corinthians, St. Paul recommends a rather strict version of the Benedict Option: "But now I am writing to you that you must not associate with anyone who claims to be a brother or sister but is sexually immoral or greedy, an idolater or slanderer, a drunkard or swindler. Do not even eat with such people."

Do not be "unequally yoked," he says in his second letter to the same group of Christians.[5] The point is that we cannot hope to be a light to the world if we get lost in the world's darkness. We cannot transform what has already transformed us. This means we must establish boundaries between ourselves and the world. We must be set apart. We modern Christians might claim that we are "in the world, not of it," but the truth is that most of us are both in and of it. We are of it because we are always in it. We never give ourselves a break from it. We give ourselves no time to think, or pray, or meditate on the deeper truths of life.

The Public School Problem

So far in this chapter I have been focusing on only one element of the problem. Christians are indoctrinated into worldly values through media and entertainment, but that is far from the only brainwashing tool at our culture's disposal. And we as adults are not the most susceptible candidates for brainwashing. The process begins much earlier. Young children are indoctrinated through media and entertainment—and through something else, something which was literally invented for the task: the public education system.

There are about fifty million kids currently enrolled in American public schools. The majority come from Christian households.[6] The problem with this should be obvious. The public school system is openly and aggressively hostile to traditional Christian values. God has been ejected from the classroom and every subject.

The goal of education should be to foster understanding. A well-educated child is a child who understands not only particular subjects like math and science, but himself, the world, and his place in it.

The one and only objective of the public school system, though, is to create the kinds of kids who will cooperate with the public school system. I don't say this is the objective of every teacher. I say this is the objective of the system itself, even if some of the teachers have loftier goals. As professor Anthony Esolen explains in his brilliant book *Out of the Ashes*, the system exists only for itself, not for any higher purpose.[7] Its objective certainly is not to impart the truth, or to prepare students for life, or to bring them closer to God or their families, or to help them understand their purpose in the world, or to do anything else that used to be defined as "education." Indeed, it necessarily does the opposite on every count—in order to fully achieve its one and only objective.

Public school is the culture a kid is immersed in for his entire young life. It is a culture that values conformity above all else. It is a culture of moral confusion. It is a culture that viciously opposes every value and priority good Christian parents want to instill in their children. The parents of public-schooled children are working at an insurmountable disadvantage. They may say to their child, *I want you to be like this and do this and believe this*, but the child is spending seven hours of his day, five days a week, nine months a year, for twelve years in an environment where nearly everyone he meets urges him to be and do and believe the opposite. Only the very rare individual can manage to endure all of that and come out as anything resembling the young adult his parents wanted him to become.

This problem becomes more and more pronounced as the schools run further and further left, away from truth and into radical progressive ideology. Many examples could be provided, but we need look no further than the matter of gender. Students are taught that "male" and "female" exist on a spectrum. A person, they are told, can fall anywhere along that increasingly widening scale, and that person's "gender identity" may ultimately bear no resemblance to his or her (or zir) biological sex. A man may be a woman, a woman may be a man, or either may choose one of the dozens of in-between options. Sometimes this deranged idea is communicated to younger students through cutesy mascots such as a "gender unicorn" or a "genderbread person."

Many schools are injecting these delusional theories into the most private spaces on campus. A female student at your local public school may have to share a bathroom or locker room with male students. She is not allowed to protest this arrangement or express any concerns at all. She will be informed that her desire for safety and privacy stems from deep-seated bigotry. This is the sort of madness that public school students must endure every day.

If we have not yet reached a point where a mass exodus from the public schools is warranted, when will that point arrive? Are we waiting until they start bringing in nude hermaphrodites to teach sex ed? I suppose even that wouldn't be enough incentive for some of us. *I can't shield my kid from what's going on out there! . . . Be in the world, not of the world! . . . Naked she-males are a part of life! . . . I can't keep him in a bubble forever! . . . He's nine years old, for God's sake!*

I realize that public school may really be the only option for some people. There are single parents of little economic means who find themselves backed into a corner where government education appears to be the only choice. And if a parent can't or won't homeschool, a private Christian education can be prohibitively expensive.

Not only that, but some Christian schools are as bad as, or worse than, the average public school. Abandoning the public school system is not an easy thing, and it presents many hurdles that may be impossible for some people to get over. The collapse of the family unit, not to mention our recent economic woes, has contributed to creating a dependence on public education. Not everyone can break free all at once, I realize.

But at this point we should all be able to agree, as Christians, that public school is not an option for those of us who have another feasible option. We should agree that public school is a matter of last resort and necessity. We should agree that public education is inherently hostile to true Christian values, and for that reason it is not even close to the ideal environment for our kids. We should agree on these points—yet, incredibly, we still don't.

I have heard it suggested that somehow the lunacy outlined above presents faith-affirming opportunities for our children, and we would actually be depriving them of something valuable if we did not give them access to those opportunities. Rationalizing parents claim that public school is a "mission field" where our kids can be "salt and light." They say that it's not fair to our kids or our communities if we "shelter" them. It's our children's duty to minister to the pagan hordes. "The system" needs our kids.

I find this point of view to be rather confused. First of all, "the system needs our kids" is a profoundly creepy statement, something a character from *Black Mirror* or *The Twilight Zone* might utter. It is not our job as parents to give the system what it needs. Even less is it our children's job. There's nothing in the Bible that says we must dedicate ourselves to maintaining a government-run education system at any cost. My first responsibility is to my family, not to the community or the school system or my kids' classmates. I will never put the interests of "the system" above those of my own children.

Whether "the system" lives or dies is not my concern. My family is my concern. I have an obligation to them, not to the local superintendent.

And if I do put my kids in "the system" for the sake of "the system," I'm not the one making the sacrifice. I'm forcing my kids to make it. At least face what you're doing. When it comes down to it, the burden of public schooling is something your child will have to shoulder, not you.

Now, yes, it is true that my kids will eventually be exposed to all kinds of strange and terrible things. As much as I'd like to keep them shielded from the evils of the world forever, I know that I can do no such thing. The question is not *whether* our kids will be exposed to this or that depravity, but *when* and *how* and *in what context*? Are you prepared to trust the school's judgment on when Junior is ready to learn about "transgenderism"—and what he is told about it?

The simple fact is that when a kid is sent to public school, he's expected to navigate and survive and thrive in a hostile, confusing, amoral environment, basically untethered from his parents. Is a child ready for that challenge by the time he's five years old? Is he ready at eight? At ten? No. Our job as parents is to "train them up in the way they should go," equip them with the armor of God, fortify them in the truth, and *then* release them into the world. That process has not been completed in conjunction with their first learning how to tie their shoes. I mean, for goodness' sake, most *adults* can't even manage to withstand the hostilities and pressures of our fallen world. And we expect little kids to do it? That's not fair to them. It's too much to ask. Way too much. They aren't equipped, they aren't ready, they aren't strong enough, and they will get eaten alive.

Let's take just this one example of the gender insanity. Our kids, in public school, will be in a world where concepts like "transgenderism" and "demigenderism" are normal, healthy, cool, and rational.

They'll be in a world where even recognizing basic biological realities is considered bigoted and oppressive. They will be in this environment literally from their first day in kindergarten. Can a child spend his entire young life in such an atmosphere and emerge on the other end with his head still on straight? It's possible, I suppose, but *you've* never had to do that. I didn't have to do that. I went to public school, but it wasn't as bad as it is now. So I would be asking my kids to live up to a spiritual and mental and moral challenge *that I myself have never endured*, and I'd be asking them to do it every day for twelve years, starting sometime around their fifth birthday.

Educational Missionaries

Your child is not ready to be a missionary. He cannot be a "witness" to others until he himself has been properly formed in the faith. It's no surprise that most of the young "missionaries" we commission and send forth to minister to the lost souls in public schools quickly become one of the lost souls. We don't need to sit around theorizing about whether the missionary approach to education is wise or effective. We already know that it isn't. The vast majority of the parents who think their kids are being "salt and light" to their peers in school are simply oblivious to the fact that their little Bible warriors have long since defected and joined the heathens. You can hardly blame the kids for this. They're just kids, after all. They *aren't* warriors. Warriors are trained and disciplined. Children are neither of those things. I imagine this is why St. Paul didn't travel to Athens and Corinth recruiting toddlers to help him carry the gospel into pagan lands.

Education is supposed to prepare a child to carry the torch of truth. That is, he's supposed to be ready to carry it *once his education has been completed*. This should not be a "throw them into the deep end to see if they can swim" strategy. They can't swim. You and I can barely swim, morally and spiritually speaking, and we're adults. Do you expect your child to be more spiritually mature and morally courageous than you?

Now, I do fully believe, ultimately, that our job is to be lights in the darkness. But a flame must first be lit, stoked, and protected before it is the bright, raging fire that we all must be if we expect to survive in this culture. Our children's education is supposed to facilitate that process, not interfere with it. Our children should be fires for Christ because of their education, not in spite of it. We can't compartmentalize the "spiritual" part of their upbringing, reserve it for evenings and weekends, and allow the lion's share of their educational experience to be dominated by humanism, hedonism, and godlessness. Education is not supposed to work that way. And it doesn't really work at all that way, as we've seen. Or, if it does work, it is only in cases where the child possesses an almost superhuman level of maturity, intelligence, and moral courage. And maybe some children really are almost superhuman in that way. But most of them aren't, yours probably aren't, and you probably aren't. That's just the reality of the situation, and we have to deal with it. I find it ironic that so many parents who expect their children to "face the reality of the world" have not faced it themselves.

It may sound like I am advocating for a country where every child is homeschooled in a house without cable or Wi-Fi. That is not what I advocate, though I wouldn't object if things did head in that direction. My proposal is much more modest. We should not leave it to the media, Hollywood, and the government (through the public school system) to shape our souls and raise our children. Our souls belong to God, and so do our children's. We have to break the grip that secular forces have over our lives so that God can rule over us again.

CHAPTER TEN

Disorganized Religion

For by one Spirit are we all baptized into one body,
whether we be Jews or Gentiles, whether we be bond or
free; and have been all made to drink into one Spirit.

—*1 Corinthians 12:13*

N
o discussion of complacent Christianity would be complete
without addressing one of the most pernicious strands of
thought infecting the church today. As secular society
increasingly rejects religion, religious society does the same. The
R-word, "religion," has taken on a negative connotation even among
those who openly confess one. Overall, one in five Americans today
identify themselves as "spiritual but not religious," and the number
of nonreligious young Americans—whether professedly "spiritual"
or not—has quadrupled in just the past three decades.

The thing that makes this trend so concerning is that you can find
it evidenced just as prominently within Christianity. According to a
recent survey, only 30 percent of Americans who don't go to church
cite a lack of religious beliefs as their reason. Most consider themselves believers, but they eschew organized church services in any

case. Many of these believers would no doubt solemnly denounce the evils of so-called "organized religion." That dreaded bogeyman has become a punching bag for the believing and the unbelieving alike.

Loving Jesus, Hating Religion

The anti–organized religion perspective was colorfully articulated a few years ago in a massively viral video made by a man named Jefferson Bethke. Titled "Why I Hate Religion, But Love Jesus," the video makes a case against the evils of organized religion in the form of spoken poetry. I cite it here because it has attracted over thirty million views and seems to generally represent the views of the average "relationship not religion" Christian. Here is a sample:

> What if I told you Jesus came to abolish religion? . . .
> I mean, if religion is so great, why has it started so many wars?
> Why does it build huge churches but fails to feed the poor? . . .
> Now back to the point—one thing is vital to mention
> How Jesus and religion are on opposite spectrums
> See, one's the work of God, but one's a man-made invention
> See, one is the cure, but the other's the infection
> See, because religion says "do"; Jesus says "done"
> Religion says "slave"; Jesus says "son"
> Religion puts you in bondage, while Jesus sets you free
> Religion makes you blind, but Jesus makes you see
> And that's why religion and Jesus are two different clans

> Religion is man searching for God; Christianity is God
> searching for man.[1]

We find here all of the standard claims against religion—thrown into a rather strained rhyme scheme. Jesus wanted to abolish religion. Religion starts wars. Religion is judgmental. Religion is rote and pointless. Religion interferes with our spiritual growth. And so on. The indictment is so standardized and universal that you might even call it a creed. Indeed, there is nothing more rote or routine, no ritual emptier, than the constant recitation of the evils of organized religion.

Chock Full o' Nots

It seems the "nonreligious" have picked up quite a few habits from the religions they despise. The Christians who reject organized religion have organized a new religion around the central tenet of disorganization. Theirs is an organized disorganized religion. Rather than defining themselves as "religious," or even (perish the thought) "organized," they define themselves as *not*. Not religious, not organized, not traditional, not orthodox. That's the problem with the new "spiritual" Christianity: it is just a big bag of nots.

Of course, there's nothing new about a Christianity that abhors organization and ritual (even as it practices both). The ancient Gnostics, the producers of such apocryphal gospels as the Gospel of Thomas and the Gospel of Philip, were staunch opponents of the burgeoning organized church. But the Gnostics also had their own theology, their own philosophies, their own system. They believed that matter is inherently evil, that Christ was wholly spirit, and that liberation can be attained through knowledge—*gnosis*. In other words, the Gnostics had the good sense to reject the organized church and everything that the church taught. The modern "spiritual"

Christians, however, borrow almost their entire theology and most of their philosophy from organized Christianity, even while claiming to be something deeper and more enlightened. They have nothing new to bring to the table. They have no special insights, no unique theological claims. They just don't like anything that smells like a rule, and they don't like going to church.

Avoiding Church

Granted, church attendance is not the most important aspect of the Christian life. But neither is it something that we should chuck to the side. Historically speaking, Christians have always met for corporate worship and prayer. Sure, as anti-church Christians point out with extreme satisfaction, the apostles didn't build cathedrals or use words like "pew" or "usher." Reliable sources inform me that the ancients didn't have coffee and doughnuts in the fellowship hall following the service, either, and they probably didn't hold annual ice cream socials. Clearly, this means our entire notion of joining together in worship on Sunday—the day the Lord rose from the dead (Matthew 28:1), the day he appeared to the apostles (John 20:26), the day he sat at table with His disciples and broke bread with them (Luke 24:30), the day of Pentecost (Acts 2:1)—is completely arbitrary.

Or maybe not. The early Christians may not have had beautiful buildings or raffle drawings at the church bazaar, but they did meet—in homes and caves and anywhere else they could manage. Acts tells us the first believers still convened for a while in synagogues to pray (Acts 2:46). As they became increasingly unwelcome there, they were forced to meet in secret. *Still, though,* they met together to worship on Sunday: "And upon the first day of the week, when the disciples came together to break bread. . . (Acts 20:7).

For hundreds of years, Christians across the known world risked torture and execution in order to come together and worship. Despite considerable danger and discomfort, they gathered—whether in tunnels or houses or wherever else—just so that they could celebrate their faith as one community, one body. Most historians believe that one of the first "official" church buildings was the Dura-Europos church in Syria, from the third century AD. Evidently, Christians all the way back then felt it necessary to have dedicated buildings for worship, even if they risked their lives by meeting there. But it wasn't until the Roman Empire declared religious tolerance in 313 that Christians could feasibly erect the sort of church structures that we would recognize today.

What about us? What makes us special? What's our excuse? Do we actually have an excuse that the Christians under Roman persecution or communist persecution or Japanese persecution or Mexican persecution or Islamic persecution didn't have? Do we have a credible and compelling reason to not do the thing that our brothers and sisters risked their lives to do? Even if we see going to church as "just" a tradition, shouldn't we have a *reason* to chuck that tradition to the side after all this time?

We do have reasons, of course. Just not very compelling ones. We're tired. It's a hassle. It's boring. The seats are uncomfortable. We have too much Facebook perusing to do. Sometimes we have justifications that feel more righteous. Maybe we went to church a while ago and something happened there that offended us. Maybe we've tried out the churches close by and found something distasteful about all of them. Someone once told me she stopped going to church because there were "rude people" and "hypocrites" at the last one she had attended. Apparently, she's looking for a church where the congregants are as flawless as she is. Perhaps next she'll search for a doctor's office where all of the patients are in perfect health when they arrive for their appointments.

The Book of Acts tells us all about the apostles traveling far and wide to convert the unbelievers and *establish churches*. They didn't come with blueprints for basilicas, but the churches they formed weren't vague and shapeless blobs. They created communities. And there were rituals and rules and laws that those communities followed. The communities were led and administered. Acts 14:23 tells us about Paul and Barnabas appointing elders in each church they formed—a completely unnecessary step if these churches were not meant to be functioning organizations. If being Christian simply means thinking nice thoughts as you snuggle with your dog, it seems the apostles wasted a lot of time on extraneous details.

In the Epistle to the Hebrews we are commanded to "meet together." In his letter to the Colossians, Paul tells us to come together for teaching, admonishment, and song. He doesn't say "in a building called a church"—largely because such buildings, as we have established, could not have existed at that time. But noticeably he also doesn't say "at home in bed by yourself" or "at the beach while you sip a daiquiri."

Most notably, Our Lord at the Last Supper spoke these words: "Do this in remembrance of me."

Now, there are two parts to "do this" that warrant further inspection. First, "do." To "do" means to perform an action. The second, "this." "This" is a word used to call attention to a certain thing or activity that is currently taking place. Put together, we have Christ instructing us to do what He was doing, and to do it together in His name. Acts tells us that the apostles proceeded to follow that instruction on the first day of each week (Acts 20:7), as they met to break bread and pray. Were those instructions only intended for the apostles? Was the Sermon on the Mount only directed at the crowd physically present to hear it?

Paul makes it even clearer: "Is not the cup of thanksgiving for which we give thanks a participation in the blood of Christ? And is not the bread that we break a participation in the body of Christ?" (1 Corinthians 10:16). Notice the words *"we"* and *"participation."*

The New Testament knows nothing of the individualized Christianity of the Christian who thinks he doesn't need an organized church. In scripture, we are referred to as a flock. We are all limbs and organs in the Body of Christ, and we are told that we cannot separate ourselves from the rest of the body. As Paul wrote, we are "baptized into one body" and must not separate ourselves from it: "And the eye cannot say unto the hand, I have no need of thee: nor again the head to the feet, I have no need of you" (1 Corinthians 12:21).

So if the fingers and hands and arms are gathering in prayer and devotion to Christ, how can the right leg stay back and mow the lawn? Has he not separated himself from the body? Has he not refused his calling to participate?

God seems to think it important to engage in active and corporate thanksgiving to Him. Scripture seems to bear that out. Paul seems to be clear. Peter and the other apostles seem to agree. Two thousand years of Christian history seem to concur. Are our excuses convincing enough to invalidate all of this?

Do they invalidate Christ's own example?

Christians who scoff at the notion of "going to some building" to pray and worship must be more enlightened than Jesus, because the New Testament frequently depicts Our Lord, a devout and observant Jew, in the Temple (Mark 1:21, Luke 2:41, and so forth) teaching and ministering. Jesus was so protective of "some building" that he physically drove the money changers out of it, incensed that they had comprised the integrity of "a house of prayer" (Matthew 21:12).

Christ believed so strongly in having a literal house of prayer—*an actual building where people gather to worship and praise God*—that

He resorted to violence to protect it. If Jesus shared the same attitude as the modern unchurched Christian, he would have been home on his couch watching Netflix (or the first-century equivalent, a Blockbuster VHS tape) and those money changers would have been spared the unpleasantness of being publicly flogged by the Son of God.

Jesus, noticeably, did not share their attitude. Neither did the apostles. Neither did the early Christians. Neither did the not-so-early Christians. The "we don't need no stinkin' church" folks are on their own, which, I guess, is how they prefer it. But there's no such thing as "on your own" Christianity. Our faith is a gift that God gave the entire world, and we are meant to share it. We are meant to experience it as a flock, as a body. And yes, as a church, *in* a church.

Religion by Any Other Name

Before we go further in our discussion of organized religion, it would probably help to define our terms. According to the *Merriam-Webster Dictionary*:

Organize: to form into a coherent unity or functioning whole.
Religion: the service and worship of God or the supernatural.[2]

It is plainly ridiculous for any Christian to profess no affiliation with religion. Christianity, literally by definition, is a religion. Call it whatever you want—a spirituality, a relationship, a pink elephant—it is still a religion. If you believe in that superhuman power we call "God," and if you believe that God has a triune nature which was summarized and explained in the opening sentences of the Gospel of John—"In the beginning was the Word, and the Word was with

God, and the Word was God"—then you are a member of the Christian religion. A Christian claiming he is not religious is like a snake professing he is not a reptile or a circle professing it is not a shape. The claim is simply nonsensical.

And Christians like Jefferson Bethke who claim that "Jesus came to abolish religion" have to reckon with the fact that the New Testament very clearly approves of it: "Religion that God our Father accepts as pure and faultless is this: to look after orphans and widows in their distress and to keep oneself from being polluted by the world" (James 1:27).

What about "organized"? As we've seen, the only option besides organized religion is disorganized religion. Rather than a system, you can have chaos. Rather than coherent unity, you can have incoherent disunity. Rather than a functioning whole, you can have dysfunctional parts. And this is indeed the option that many Christians have chosen. As a result, there are hundreds of sects, thousands of denominations, and countless versions of what Christianity is supposed to mean. Put a hundred random American Christians into a room and you probably won't find a majority consensus on any topic whatsoever. We have certainly succeeded in being disorganized, but I haven't noticed any of the spiritual enlightenment and devotional depth that was supposed to flow from our bold rejection of unity and coherence.

Rejecting Ritual

It's true that so-called "organized religion" is ritualistic. This fact is often used as an argument against it. But there is nothing fundamentally wrong with ritual. Indeed, it is quite natural. Human beings are inherently ritualistic. Those who have dispensed with Christian rituals still engage in dozens or even hundreds of rituals every day. They brush their teeth, they gather around watercoolers at work, they shake hands when they greet people, they watch TV at night, they eat dinner with their families. They spend their whole lives following protocols and social customs. They perform dozens of ceremonial acts every day without realizing it. This is why organized religion is ritualistic—because human beings are ritualistic.

The Christian religion is not "man-made"—unless the "man" to whom we are referring when we use that term is Christ—but it is made *for* man. And man is a creature moved by ritual, music, beauty, art, and community. Man is also a creature in need of direction and clarity because he is a creature prone to rebellion and confusion. That is why organized religion exists. It is not perfect because it is not only made for man but, by unfortunate necessity, run by him. But it is wholly preferable to any other available option.

The Church Militant

Ultimately, Christianity must be "organized" for the same reason, and in almost the same way, that an army is organized. It is not fashionable these days to encourage militant religion. It is even less popular to urge a holy war. But as Christians, we are indeed soldiers of Christ, and we are indeed involved in a holy war—one of spiritual combat, not physical violence. We cannot charge into battle haphazard and disorganized. It is better for us to operate from the same battle plan. C. S. Lewis puts the matter in clever and eloquent terms: "Enemy-occupied territory—that's what this world is. Christianity is the story of how the rightful king has landed, you might say landed in disguise, and is calling us all to take part in a great campaign of sabotage. When you go to church you are really listening in to the secret wireless from our friends: that is why the enemy is so anxious to prevent us from going."[3]

I have never heard of a "great campaign of sabotage" that succeeded on the basis of disorganization. And I certainly have never heard of a military unit—and that is what we are as Christians—that finds any advantage in denying that it is a military unit. I think, especially in these dark times, it is important that we embrace the militant, warrior spirit of Christianity. It is a spirit that has an ancient history, and it is not a history of which we should be ashamed. We should own it proudly, now more than ever.

St. Paul wrote to the Ephesians, "Put on the full armor of God, so that you can take your stand against the devil's schemes. For our struggle is not against flesh and blood, but against the rulers, against the authorities, against the powers of this dark world and against the spiritual forces of evil in the heavenly realms" (Ephesians 6:11–12).

In 1095, Pope Urban II launched the First Crusade—a just war, a war of defense of Middle Eastern Christians against Muslim conquest and persecution, despite what your public school teacher may have told you. He spoke these words to the crusaders he had commissioned:

> With what reproaches will the Lord overwhelm us if you do not aid those who, with us, profess the Christian religion! Let those who have been accustomed unjustly to wage private warfare against the faithful now go against the infidels and end with victory this war which should have been begun long ago. Let those who for a long time, have been robbers, now become knights. Let those who have been fighting against their brothers and relatives now fight in a proper way against the barbarians. Let those who have been serving as mercenaries for small pay now obtain the eternal reward. Let those who have been wearing themselves out in both body and soul now work for a double honor. Behold! on this side will be the sorrowful and poor, on that, the rich; on this side, the enemies of the

Lord, on that, his friends. Let those who go not put off the journey, but rent their lands and collect money for their expenses; and as soon as winter is over and spring comes, let them eagerly set out on the way with God as their guide.[4]

If only there were someone to issue a similar speech and launch another crusade today. What we need in our culture is a spiritual crusade, where we wield the weapons of prayer and faith and truth. And if such a crusade is ever to be launched, and if it is to have any chance of success, we need indeed to be organized in our religion.

CHAPTER ELEVEN

Cheap Repentance

*From that time Jesus began to preach, "Repent, for the
kingdom of heaven is at hand."*

—*Matthew 4:17*

The good news is that God is merciful. I can't imagine what a
dreary hell life would be if He were not. Surely we'd all be
doomed. And you couldn't really blame God if that were the
case. It's not as though we could ever deserve His mercy or get ourselves into a position where we no longer need it. We'll always need
it, and we'll always receive it, if only we open our hearts to it.

This is, without a doubt, the most sensational and illogical thing
about the Christian faith. It's not that hard to believe in a God who
created the heavens and earth and passed down laws for His creatures
to follow—every religion throughout history has taught something
like that. But a God who would constantly forgive the insubordinate,
ungrateful, selfish, lazy little brats who populate this planet? A God
who would even send His own Son here to die an agonizing death
on the cross for the sake of those who nailed Him to it? A God who

could hold the cosmos in the palm of his hand and yet would humble Himself in front of puny, ridiculous mortals like us? A God larger and more powerful than the universe itself, yet who knelt and washed the feet of His disciples? Well, that's something else entirely. It's hard to swallow. Hard for me, anyway.

An Incomprehensible Mercy

Of all the Christian doctrines, I find the doctrine of God's perfect mercy the most difficult to believe, in the sense that it takes the most effort for me to believe it. But my difficulty in fully accepting this essential teaching of our faith stems from my own weakness, not a weakness in the teaching. Indeed, while the teaching is incredible and unlike anything you find in any other religion, it does make sense.

It is only out of an eternal abundance of love that an all-powerful cosmic being would create human life in the first place. If He created life for any other purpose and with any other motivation, He would have realized His mistake and wiped us from the planet long ago. The fact that we're here after millennia of greed, violence, and corruption tells us that God simply loves us, and that's all there is to the story. But a perfect being could not love such imperfect beings without an infinite supply of mercy. One could argue that He would not be a perfect being if He lacked mercy. So the fact that He is perfectly merciful is consistent and easy to understand on an intellectual level.

Yet I struggle with God's infinite mercy because, I think, I so lack mercy that I can't really understand what it is or how it works. I know that I'm a wretched, disloyal servant, and that I have gotten so little accomplished, and that I bring such a meager offering to the table, and so I struggle to accept the idea that God would accept me. I struggle because I wouldn't accept me. If someone spit in my face as many times as I've spit in God's, I don't think I could forgive them. And because I am so lacking in this virtue, I can't begin to wrap my head around God's perfect manifestation of it.

I'm not sure that I have ever in my life shown mercy to anyone, even if I've shown what may appear to be mercy. My mercy, my forgiveness, must always be arrived at by a process of rationalization. I can forgive someone but I have to justify the forgiveness. I have to find some positive quality in that person, I have to tell myself that he deserves it, I have to convince myself that his offense against me wasn't as bad as I made it out to be. Only after that torturous intellectual exercise can I extend what many would consider to be mercy. But it's not mercy. It's simply me choosing to move on from something because I've talked myself into moving on from it on faulty grounds.

In truth, he may not deserve it, and there may be very few positive qualities in him, and his slight against me may have been just as bad as, if not worse than, what I made it out to be. True mercy would be to *recognize* these facts and yet forgive anyway. A man is only merciful if he forgives the unforgivable, just as a man is only courageous if he acts with bravery in spite of his fear. A man who feels no fear cannot be brave, because his bravery is contingent on his lack of fear. A man who tricks himself into seeing imaginary positive qualities in another person cannot be merciful, because his mercy is contingent on those false qualities. Mercy is only mercy if it is entirely undeserved. You might say that mercy is the act of giving someone what he *doesn't* deserve. A person who slaps you in the face deserves a slap in return, but Christ tells us to turn the other cheek and show him a patience and a kindness he is not owed.

It's necessary that we do this because it's what we need God to do for us: "The measure you use, it will be measured to you"(Matthew 7:2). If we use a justice-based measure for other people, we have damned ourselves, because God will subject us to the same scrutiny. He will give us what we deserve, and what we all deserve is Hell. Because we are sinners, Hell is our natural destiny. It is only by supernatural means that we escape it. St. Paul says, "The wages of sin is death, but the gift of God is eternal life in Christ Jesus our Lord" (Romans 6:23). A man's wages are what is due to him. A gift is something added, beyond and greater than what's due.

It's common to hear people say, "I just want what I deserve" or "I want what is owed to me," but they mean something close to the opposite. Whatever suffering or deprivation they're complaining about when they utter those phrases—and worse—is exactly what they deserve. What they really want is to be granted a joy they are not entitled to and do not warrant. They want to be given that which is not due to them.

A False Self-Esteem

It's important that our inherent unworthiness be established and understood if we want to fully appreciate the depth of God's mercy. This is one of the reasons why I've always been uncomfortable with the modern doctrine of "self-esteem," especially as it has crept into our churches. It is fundamentally anti-Christian to insist that people always feel good about themselves. One cannot preach the true gospel and the gospel of self-acceptance simultaneously. In reality there is plenty within us that is unacceptable and that we ought to despise. We must confront these aspects of ourselves or we will never repent of them.

The people with what we call "low self-esteem" have low self-esteem for good reason. Most of what they hate about themselves they ought to hate. Most of the flaws they find in their hearts really are flaws, and they should be troubled by them. It's the people with "high self-esteem" who suffer from hallucinations. They develop this "esteem" for themselves by ignoring or rationalizing the parts of them that are most certainly not worthy of esteem.

To hold something in "esteem" is to regard it highly. But why should you regard yourself highly? You're weak. You're a coward. You're a sinner. Face it. You must face it, or you'll never be cured of it. Your self-esteem is unwarranted and fanciful. You may as well put on a crown and call yourself the Queen of England. Your esteem for yourself is that delusional, if not more so.

The right approach is to hold God in high esteem, the highest esteem, and recognize that our positive attributes, what few we have, are granted to us by the grace of God. We ought to take no pride in them. A spirit of gratitude, not "self-esteem," is what we should cultivate. A Christian who is truly at peace is not one who has self-esteem, but one with an overabundant sense of gratitude to God. As for himself, he knows that he's a shameful sinner, but he rejoices in God's love and presence. Esteem for the Divine is confused with esteem for the Self by people who have never learned the difference between the two.

The only aspects of ourselves that we can really take ownership of—the parts that do not come from God—are the negatives. And we have no right to ignore those or "accept" them in an effort to be the kind of confident, well-adjusted person that self-help books tell us we should be. Those negatives—and they are plentiful—are truly awful, truly hideous, truly outrageous and wicked. We should not despair on account of them, but neither should we overlook them. What we should do is face them, understand them, and bring them before God with a contrite and penitent heart. We don't say to God, *Check me out, Lord. I'm so great!* Rather, we say, *Forgive me, Lord, for I am ugly and wretched.* And through that repentance we begin to experience God's mercy in its fullness.

The Necessity of Repentance

We cannot separate mercy from repentance. The problem is that many churches try to do exactly that. It was decided at some point in the last fifty years that churches were focused too intently on fire, brimstone, and repentance. Maybe they were. Surely, our faith lives shouldn't be consumed by guilt and fear. But in modern times we have run all the way to the other extreme. Now we imagine that our faith in God actually insulates us from guilt. We imagine that repentance is unimportant, or even entirely unnecessary.

We went from obsessing too much over the prospect of damnation to pretending that we're not at risk of suffering it. I think, if we must err, we're better erring on the other end of the spectrum. Better to feel too much guilt for your sin than none. Better to be too afraid of Hell than not at all. Better to be overly zealous in your repentance than never to repent in the first place.

"Work out your salvation with fear and trembling," St. Paul tells the Philippians (2:12). To which the modern Christian says, *Dude, chill.* I think we'd be safer adopting St. Paul's approach. What reaction can we have *but* fear and trembling when we honestly confront the vileness of our sin? How many of us have even attempted such a confrontation?

Anyone who has not felt revulsion and fear at himself has either never sinned or never faced the fact that he does. We can be sure we do not belong to the first category, which leaves only the second. And if we haven't faced our sin, how can we say we've repented of it? It's not enough to casually yawn, roll our eyes, and mutter to God dismissively, *Sorry for the bad stuff I'm doing, whatever it is.* We wouldn't accept that sort of apology from our own kids, so why should God accept it from His? How could He? He can't force us to be sincerely penitent any more than He can force us to sincerely love Him. He can give us the grace, and He has, but we have to submit.

Blind to Sin

There are Christians today who will outright declare that repentance is not necessary at all because God "doesn't see our sin." They view the atonement as some kind of great curtain that has dropped down from the sky and hidden our sin backstage, out of God's view. But this is the wrong way of looking at it, for a number of reasons.

First, when this view chucks repentance to the side, it also discards forgiveness. We are told of God's forgiveness over and over again in scripture—not as a onetime event, but as an ongoing process: "And when you stand praying, if you hold anything against anyone, forgive them, so that your Father in heaven may forgive you your sins" (Mark 11:25). How can our Father in Heaven forgive trespasses that He cannot see? If God cannot see sin, He cannot forgive sin.

Second, if God "can't see our sin" then He is not omniscient. Scripture tells us that we "all are naked and exposed" before a God (Hebrews 4:13) who "sees everything under the heavens" (Job 28:24). If He cannot see our sin, then we are not in any sense naked before Him, and He certainly cannot see everything under the heavens. Considering how often we sin, it would seem that He can see almost nothing at all if He cannot see sin.

Third, this is a misunderstanding of the nature of the atonement. Through Christ, God "reconciled the world to himself" (2 Corinthians 5:19). He did not blind Himself in the process. He told us to pluck out our eyes rather than sin. He did not promise that He would pluck out His own eyes if we continue sinning. Neither did He agree to turn around and look the other way for the rest of time. We were redeemed and set free from the bondage of sin. That is the essence of the greatest miracle in the history of the world. But in our freedom, we are free to run back into bondage. The slave may be rescued from his captors, and he may wander back into their clutches again if he is reckless with his freedom. And it is when we find ourselves back under that yoke, wearing the rusty yet strangely comfortable chains of sin once again, that we must cry out to God in repentance.

There is a reason why "Repent and believe" was the very first message Christ preached, His first homily (Mark 1:15). There is a reason why repentance was Paul's message, and Peter's message, and John the Baptist's message, and the message of all the prophets who came before them. It is because repentance is the first step. Christ cried out for repentance with His first steps into public ministry because it must be our first step as Christians. And not just our first step when we initially become Christian. It must be our first step every time we approach God. We can get nowhere in our walk if we do not begin by asking for God's forgiveness.

Hand on the Stove

The real problem with repentance, at least in the modern mind, is that it must inevitably involve shame. We have developed a deep aversion to shame, but little aversion to the sin that causes it. We say that we should be free of shame as Christians, and we are partly right. We should be free from shame as far as our faith is concerned. St. Paul triumphantly declares that he is "unashamed of the Gospel" (Romans 1:16). He makes no such declaration about his sin. Indeed, clearly he was ashamed of it: "I do not understand what I do. For what I want to do I do not do, but what I hate I do" (Romans 7:15). There is that word again: hate. He hates what he does. He is ashamed of it. And in that shame, he repents and is forgiven.

Shame is like the stinging, fiery pain we feel when we put our hand on a hot stove. Trying to remove shame without giving up sin is like trying to remove the pain in your hand without removing your hand from the stove. Repentance is a two-step process. The first is to take your hand off the stove and turn from your sin. The second is to turn to God and resolve that you will try your hardest never to commit that same sin again. We can finally be relieved of the shame of that sin when we have amended our ways through God's grace.

If we refuse to feel any shame, then we refuse to repent. And if we refuse to repent, then we cannot be reconciled with God. Forgiveness may be a one-way street, but reconciliation is not. God offers forgiveness to us free of charge, as the bill has already been paid. But we must accept His forgiveness through humble repentance. Fortunately, Our Lord does not leave us in any confusion about how repentance works and what it looks like. He illustrated the process through one of His greatest parables: the prodigal son.

Repentance Illustrated

You remember the story. The son has an inheritance coming to him from his father, much as we do from our Father. The important thing to remember about an inheritance is that it isn't earned by the person who receives it. The inheritance belongs to the father, accrued through his own efforts, and only because he loves his children is he prepared to share it with them. But, much like us, the son doesn't want to wait to cash in his portion. He finds the idea of staying at home, doing chores, living in obedience, and waiting for his reward unappealing. He goes to his father and asks to be given everything now so that he can spend it as he sees fit.

One can't help but think that this guy is quite the piece of work. What sort of person asks his dad for his inheritance money ahead of time so that he can leave home and blow it all on hookers? It seems unthinkable, and it is, but it's exactly what we're doing when we choose to sin. We're saying to God, *I don't want to work and obey and wait patiently to receive the rewards of Heaven at the time you appoint. I want to have my happiness now, even if it means there will be no happiness left for me when the appointed time arrives. I'd rather have a few fleeting moments of pleasure instead of an eternity of joy. Let me free from your grasp so that I can go and do what I wish.*

Unthinkable, indeed. And God, just like the father in the parable, will respect our wishes. He won't lock us in or tie us down to prevent us from leaving Him. He wants us to be at home with Him of our own free will. He doesn't want slaves who only serve Him because of the shackles around their ankles.

So, the son goes off and very quickly squanders everything. Eventually he finds himself unhappier than he was before, with no reward to look forward to, living in squalor, longing to eat and be treated even as well as the swine he tends. After he had forsaken his father for the sake of the world, the world in turn had forsaken him. He opted for immediate pleasure over a deeper joy, and ended up with neither.

It was only after all of this—after he had blown all his money, after he'd felt starvation and destitution, after he'd been rejected by everyone—that he made up his mind to return home. Again, we can feel nothing but disgust at this stupid, selfish man. He had to be reduced to the level of a pig before he began to rethink his course of action. And even then, the revelation was not immediate. We're told he was only down in the mud with the pigs because he had hired himself out to someone from that country. He was willing, for a time, to debase himself, working for someone who treated him as less than human rather than simply going home, where he had responsibilities but also a father who loved him, food to eat, and a warm bed to sleep in. He actively embraced his own misery. Ironically, he humiliated himself out of pride. What sort of person does that? I mean, aside from me and you.

Notice what happens next. He leaves everything behind—admittedly not a very impressive feat, considering he has nothing, anyway—and returns home. The effort he makes here is minuscule in comparison to the months or years he had spent wasting his father's fortune on prostitutes, but it was a necessary effort all the same. Nothing we can ever do will of itself compensate for or negate our sin, but that doesn't excuse us from the obligation to act. The prodigal son didn't earn his place at his father's house by renouncing his old ways and making the journey home, but he wouldn't have had a place had he not done so. We don't earn our entrance into Heaven by repenting and actively coming back to Christ, but still we must repent and come back or we will not enter.

And note the speech the son has planned upon his arrival: "Father, I have sinned against Heaven and against you. I am not worthy to be called your son. Make me like one of your hired servants" (Luke 15:18–19). He returns in total humility, expecting nothing, feeling entitled to nothing. He throws himself at the mercy of his father, acknowledging that he is not worthy of forgiveness, and that by his betrayal he rightfully forfeited his place at his father's table and ought to be disowned and shunned. His only petition is that his father may permit him to sleep out in the shed with the servants. This is the sort of contrition that is necessary for forgiveness. We cannot fully receive God's mercy if there is even the slightest bit of calculation or self-interest in our repentance. We cannot fully receive His mercy if we do not acknowledge just how badly we need it and how little we deserve it.

Yet his father saw him walking up the path and ran out to greet him. The son didn't even have to make it all the way home. His father

saw that he intended to come home, and that he had already jour-
neyed part of the way. He didn't stand coldly at the door and wait for
his son to travel up the path, walking alone and in shame. He rushed
to him and hugged him. His father was so overflowing with love for
his son, and so distraught over having lost him, that he wasted no
time. He wanted only to embrace him and celebrate his return. Prepare a feast, he said. Put a robe on his back and a ring on his finger.
Rejoice.

Our Lord holds no grudge against us. He doesn't stand off to the
side, sullen and disenchanted by our failures and betrayals. Upon our
return, He doesn't cross His arms and hiss, *Oh, it's you. Well, now you
come back*—in the way that we act towards others in similar situations. Often when we are wronged, even if the person is sincerely
regretful, we still require that he suffer some additional shame as
recompense for the evil committed against us. We aren't happy simply to be reconciled. We need to settle the score. We want the debt to
be paid. Our Lord does not share this attitude. He knows that nothing we do can ever settle the score, which is why He died for us, to
do what we cannot. All He wants from us now is a sincere and contrite heart.

But while this heartwarming scene is unfolding, the other son,
the faithful one, is filled with resentment. You can really see where
he's coming from, can't you? Here he's been slaving away all his life,
doing everything that has been asked of him, and never has his father
thrown a celebration in his honor. Yet the prodigal brother comes
waltzing back after all this time spent doing God knows what, and
his father practically throws a parade. *Where's my parade? Where's
my fatted calf? Where's my robe and my ring? It's unfair,* he thinks. And
he's right. It is unfair.

His brother doesn't deserve this kind treatment, that's true. But
he doesn't deserve it, either. The very fact that the faithful brother

has made this joyous occasion all about himself only proves that he's not quite the selfless, loyal son that he imagines himself to be. By his words he reveals that much of his so-called "obedience" has been calculated and self-serving. He demands recognition and reward beyond what his father's love and generosity has already provided him. His father could have cast him out into the street at the first sign of this haughtiness and arrogance, and he would have been justified in doing so. His father could have said, *Everything that I own belongs to you, but if that's not good enough, go out and earn what you can for yourself. See how far that gets you.* That would have been fair, after all.

It's not fair for anyone to be given what is not his, yet our Father opens up eternal joy to us, despite the fact that it isn't rightfully ours and we've done nothing to earn it or deserve it. This knowledge should make us eternally grateful for any blessing, however small, and totally accepting of any suffering, however large, knowing that it's only the smallest portion of the suffering we're due. But too often we vacillate between the positions of these two brothers. One moment we're mortgaging everything and risking our eternal salvation for some small pleasure, and the next we're demanding that a thousand trumpets resound from on high in recognition of some small act of charity and fidelity—thereby draining the act of all of its charity and fidelity. We are so fickle, so self-centered, so focused on ourselves. And yet God is always there, standing by the door, ready to run out and greet us upon our return.

CHAPTER TWELVE

Heaven for Everyone

*And I heard a loud voice from the throne saying, "Look!
God's dwelling place is now among the people, and he
will dwell with them. They will be his people, and God
himself will be with them and be their God. 'He will wipe
every tear from their eyes. There will be no more death' or
mourning or crying or pain, for the old order of things has
passed away." He who was seated on the throne said, "I am
making everything new."*

—Revelation 21:3–5

I will be accused of writing a bleak and despairing book. But I
think this has been a book *about* despair, not a book *of* despair.
The Christian existentialist Søren Kierkegaard thought of despair
as a falling out of alignment with God. Despair is when finite beings
give up on, reject, the infinite aspects of reality and themselves. In
that sense, our culture is deep in despair, and our church has followed it into that same pit. That's the story I have tried to tell in these
pages.

What is the antidote? Well, hope is the opposite of despair. And
Christianity, in its truest form, at its authentic core, is a deeply hopeful religion. It discovers purpose in suffering. It grasps at beauty

amidst hardship. It rejects despair and condemns it as one of the gravest sins. The Christian faith plunges into the darkness and finds Christ there, healing the sick and driving out demons. It tells us to come to Christ with our weariness and rest in Him (Matthew 11:28). It tells us to give up our anxieties and worries (Matthew 6:34). It tells us to rejoice and be glad for the days God has given us (Psalm 118).

Even in the darkest moment of scripture, even on Calvary, there is tenderness and light. Our Lord entrusts His mother to John, and John to His mother, then He turns to the penitent thief and promises eternal life. Joy on the cross. Hope in death. This is the essence of the Christian faith. Hope springs eternal, as Alexander Pope once wrote.

But we complacent Christians have lost sight of the eternal hope. We talk about the need to be hopeful, we like the idea of hope, but our hope lies in things temporal. We hope for comfort and pleasure along the road. We have hopes for the day, hopes for the year, maybe even "long-term" hopes for things five or ten years down the road. But all of our hopes have expiration dates. We are constantly achieving our meager and temporary hopes, finding that they do not satisfy, and then scrambling to conjure a new hope, a new purpose, a new source of satisfaction.

The church in America seems to go to great lengths to foster this short-term attitude. We have already seen how Hell is rarely mentioned from the pulpit. But Heaven, too, seems to make only cameo appearances. Christians are encouraged to focus on more immediate and practical concerns. We are told to strive for social justice, a fair economic system, reductions in poverty and homelessness, racial harmony, and so on. These are fine goals, as far as they go, but the trouble is that they do not go very far. We cannot pin our ultimate hope on these things.

These problems can and should be addressed, but they can never be solved. "The poor you will always have with you," Our Lord assures us in Matthew 26:11. And even if poverty and the rest of the world's ills could be solved, we would only have succeeded in making the earth a more comfortable place for the seventy or eighty years that any one of us will be around to enjoy it. Those few decades wither away into dust in the face of eternity. Our hope must be rooted in the next life, not—as Joel Osteen would have it—our "best life."[1] We can only enter into the eternal joy of Heaven if we truly desire it. This, I think, is the definition of hope. Hope is more than mere optimism or happy thoughts or sunny dispositions. Hope, at its most fundamental level, is a desire for things eternal.

A Crisis of Desire

This, in the end, is what makes our complacent and cowardly Christianity so dangerous. Blithely sauntering along the broad road that leads to destruction (see Matthew 7:13), we are too satiated, too pampered, too distracted and preoccupied, to develop a true and insatiable yearning for an eternal union with God. The crisis in our culture is a crisis of hopelessness because it is a crisis of desire. We want too much and not enough at the same time. We desire too many things and the wrong things.

In *The Brothers Karamazov*, Dostoevsky has Father Zosima say this about desire in the modern world: "The world has proclaimed the reign of freedom, especially of late, but what do we see in this freedom of theirs? Nothing but slavery and self-destruction! For the world says: 'You have desires and so satisfy them, for you have the same rights as the most rich and powerful. Don't be afraid of satisfying them and even multiply your desires.'"

The multiplication of desires. This is what our culture has given us. It gives us things and the desire for those things. And the more attached we are to things—whether those things are physical objects, or sins, or pets, or people—the less we hunger for the real bread of eternal life (see John 6:55). We are like a man dying of malnutrition despite having a pantry full of food. He stuffed himself with soda and chips and chocolate, but it wasn't enough. It couldn't sustain him. And he never felt the hunger pains because he had filled his stomach with junk.

Every petty and meaningless desire of ours is filled. We have so much that we even invent new desires and fulfill them, too. Every day you hear about some new fetish, some new perverse interest that has taken hold of some segment of society. And with these new fetishes always come new "rights." We plunge into ourselves and bring to the surface every dark and depraved and strange desire we can find, and then we fight for the right to satisfy it. We not only indulge ourselves, we even feel heroic in our indulgence. We have made selfishness into a cause; a banner under which we march and sing songs of victory.

All of it is empty, none of it has any substance, but we drown our souls in it, in this sea of nothingness, and God is pushed ever further to the periphery. As Jeremiah said, we have gone after empty idols and become empty ourselves; we have exchanged our glory for useless things (Jeremiah 2:5, 2:11). Our lives have become consumed by so much noise, so much commotion, so much food, so much media, so many advertisements, so many lights and sounds, and all it does is keep us focused on a million things besides the one thing that matters. We run from God into the haze of modern culture, and we lose Him somewhere in the chaos, in the noise.

Blessed Are Those Who Suffer

It is clear why scripture says that Christians "glory in our sufferings" (Romans 5:3). The one who suffers is truly blessed. If the core of the true Christian life is joy through suffering, then the antithesis of the Christian life is joy in the avoidance of suffering. A man who has had only comfort and has never really allowed himself to suffer is in a perilous state. And it is in exactly this state that the American Christian lives, and dies, and is damned.

But a man who endures the worst deprivation, the most agonizing personal loss, the most tragic misfortune, the harshest persecution, is granted a monumental opportunity in his agony. He is given what most of us on the broad and comfortable road to perdition will never face: an abrupt and distinct choice between God and despair. A clear moment of choosing.

Now that all he loves has been ripped from him, now that he is miserable, now that the frivolous pleasures that life offers him seem suddenly stupid and useless or entirely out of reach, now that he is poor and pitiful and wretched, he can do one of two things. He can realize that the Lord is his only refuge and his only comfort, and fall to his knees right there in the darkness, crying out like the blind man who met Christ on the way to Jericho, "Jesus, son of David, have mercy on me!" (see Mark 10:47). And he can live from then on clutching desperately to his Savior's robes as if he will surely fall forever into the abyss if he loosens his grip for even a moment. He can find himself so radically determined to enter through the narrow gate that he will hack off whatever parts of himself may prevent him from fitting through it. He can lose everything and realize that his only solace is to gain eternity.

Or he can lash out in hatred against God and retreat into himself. He can resign himself to despair. He can try to heal his misery by making himself more miserable. Perhaps he will stick with that plan for the rest of his life and be lost. But there is still a good chance that, after having chosen the wrong path, he will reverse course and find salvation. As long as he hates God, he is only a moment away from loving Him. That is the startling and drastic choice God gave this man: hate Me or love Me.

If he does not choose to love God, he must surely hate Him. He could not possibly remain neutral on the subject. He will either praise God as his only comfort and salvation, or he will curse Him as a Divine Tyrant and the Author of all his misery. No matter what, his feelings towards Him will be intense. Even if he feels hatred, that is exactly the kind of raw material that the Holy Spirit can take and mold into love.

Necessary Desperation

Most of us are not so fortunate as to suffer misfortune. We reject God, but we reject Him gradually. We have all of our petty comforts and self-indulgences with us along the way, and those comforts keeps us from noticing which road we have taken. We never come to hate God, but neither do we come love Him. We come, instead, to a state of spiritual indifference. We just don't take Him into consideration. We imagine that this is good enough because at least we don't hate Him. But in Revelation 3:15 He tells us the very opposite: "I wish that you were hot or cold." It is better to scream at God in hatred every day than to never think about Him at all. It is better to give God something real and powerful to work with—even if it is hatred, anger, and misery—than to give him nothing but shrugs and yawns.

Those who came to Christ in the Gospels were nearly panicked in their desperation: The woman who grabbed at His garments in the crowd. The paralytic who was lowered through a hole in the roof. The blind man who followed Jesus, shouting after Him to have mercy on him. The wealthy man who climbed a tree to see over the crowd. The woman bathing His feet with her tears. The centurion who asked that only one word be spoken so that his servant would be healed.

What binds all of these pitiful characters together is that they wanted nothing more than to see Christ, make contact with Him, speak to Him, beseech Him. And they got what they so badly wanted—precisely because they so badly wanted it. The bar is not set very high at all. God does not expect much of us, really. He wants us to want Him. Once we do, everything else is easier. Even our crosses sit lightly on our shoulders. Our burden becomes easy, our yoke light.

Not Everyone Wants Heaven

This is the simple truth of the Christian walk and of salvation. Christ is there for anyone who really wants Him. Heaven is open to anyone who actually wants to go. But we only want to go to Heaven if we want a life that is completely consumed by Christ and nothing else. If we want a life that is only partly Christ, we don't want Heaven. We may as well admit it now while there's still time.

If Christ is not close to our primary joy in life, how can we go to a place where He is the *only* joy? If we are content to make Christ only a part of our lives here, how can we go to a place where there is no life apart from Him? I ask these questions of myself before I ask them of anyone else. I certainly know that my life doesn't revolve entirely around Christ at present, but the more important question I must face is this: Do I want it to?

Many of us think we desire Heaven because we imagine it as a place of self-centered pleasure. We believe that the happiness of Heaven is much like the happiness we find on earth. So if we enjoy eating good food, watching movies, playing sports, whatever, we fantasize that Heaven will be like some sort of resort where we can eat all the cheesecake we want and have access to an infinite Netflix library and maybe toss the pigskin around with Johnny Unitas on a football field in the clouds. But if this is the only kind of happiness we desire—a selfish, indulgent kind of happiness—then we clearly do not desire the happiness of Heaven.

John Henry Newman once suggested that our attitude towards church is a pretty good indication of how much we really desire Heaven, and how much we would actually enjoy it if we went there:

> Heaven then is not like this world; I will say what it is much more like,—*a church*. For in a place of public worship no language of this world is heard; there are no schemes brought forward for temporal objects, great or small; no information how to strengthen our worldly interests, extend our influence, or establish our credit. These things indeed may be right in their way, [as long as] we do not set our hearts upon them; still (I repeat), it is certain that we hear nothing of them in a church. Here we hear solely and entirely of *God*. We praise Him, worship Him, sing to Him, thank Him, confess to Him, give ourselves up to Him, and ask His blessing. And *therefore*, a church is like heaven; viz. because both in the one and the other, there is one single sovereign subject—religion—brought before us.
>
> Supposing, then, instead of it being said that no irreligious man could serve and attend on God in heaven (or see Him, as the text expresses it), we were told that no irreligious man could worship, or spiritually see Him in church; should we not at once perceive the meaning of the doctrine? viz. that, were a man to come hither, who had suffered his mind to grow up in its own way, as nature or chance determined, without any deliberate habitual effort after truth and purity, he would find no real pleasure here, but would soon get weary of the place; because, in this house of God, he would hear only of that one subject which

he cared little or nothing about, and nothing at all of those things which excited his hopes and fears, his sympathies and energies. If then a man without religion (supposing it possible) were admitted into heaven, doubtless he would sustain a great disappointment. Before, indeed, he fancied that he could be happy there; but when he arrived there, he would find no discourse but that which he had shunned on earth, no pursuits but those he had disliked or despised, nothing which bound him to aught *else* in the universe, and made him feel at home, nothing which he could enter into and rest upon. He would perceive himself to be an isolated being, cut away by Supreme Power from those objects which were still entwined around his heart. Nay, he would be in the presence of that Supreme Power, whom he never on earth could bring himself steadily to think upon, and whom now he regarded only as the destroyer of all that was precious and dear to him. Ah! he could not *bear* the face of the Living God; the Holy God would be no object of joy to him. "Let us alone! What have we to do with thee?" is the sole thought and desire of unclean souls, even while they acknowledge His majesty. None but the holy can look upon the Holy One; without holiness no man can endure to see the Lord.

When, then, we think to take part in the joys of heaven without holiness, we are as inconsiderate as if we supposed we could take an interest in the worship of Christians here below without possessing it in our measure. A careless, a sensual, an unbelieving mind, a mind destitute of the love and fear of God, with narrow views and earthly aims, a low standard of duty, and a benighted conscience, a mind contented with itself, and unresigned to God's will, would feel as little pleasure, at the last day, at the words, "Enter into the joy of thy Lord," as it does now at the words, "Let us pray." Nay, much less, because, while we are in a church, we may turn our thoughts to other subjects, and contrive to forget that God is looking on us; but that will not be possible in heaven.[2]

As Newman points out, we cannot expect to find happiness in Heaven if we detest going to church, praying, and reading the Bible. If we find religion to be a crashing bore and are stimulated only by what is selfish and secular, how do we think we'll fare in a place where the only things we really love are obliterated, and the one thing we always avoid must now be the center of our existence forever?

If all the things that are purely about God in this life are dull and uninteresting to us, and all we do is bide our time until we can get back to the TV, then Heaven would be torture. There would be no leaving God to get back to the TV. It would be only God always. If we find little appeal in spending even a few minutes with God now, how can we expect that we'll find any appeal in spending infinity with Him?

This is the problem with people who say they don't pray, attend church, or read scripture, but go on walks instead, or spend time with their families, or go to the beach, and that's where they "find God." It's true that God can be found in all of those things, but you can also enjoy them without thinking about God at all. There are only a few activities in life that are purely, solely, and inevitably about God and God only, and those are the activities many Christians enjoy least of all. Most of us can't stand to worship the Lord unless it's in the context of some relaxing and entertaining recreational activity, yet we still claim to desire Heaven.

No, it's not Heaven we want. It's a vacation.

This is the reason Christ tells us to give up everything and follow Him—because we have to get ourselves accustomed to living in a way that is hinged entirely on God. For people like me, to find joy in such an existence takes practice. To desire God above all else requires spiritual exercise and conditioning. If you think you're already in the right condition, here's a good test: Drop to your knees when you get home tonight and pray. Tell me how long you last before you need to pick up your phone to scroll Facebook. I imagine if you get to the three-minute mark, you're way above average. Can those of us who only tolerate prayer in half-hearted 180-second spurts seriously claim that we want nothing more than to be in communion with the Lord for *eternity*? Of course not.

So the solution, I think, is to work at becoming the sort of people who find joy in what is holy and sacred. It's not a matter of "earning" Heaven—that price has been paid—rather, it's a matter of conditioning ourselves for it. The souls in Hell are only in Hell because they're in no condition for Heaven. It's not just a bunch serial killers and rapists down there, after all. There are also the regular people who loved themselves more than God and preferred their own enjoyment to worshipping and serving Him.

A God Who Waits

The good news is that God is exceedingly patient. He fans the flame of spiritual desire within us for as long as it takes to turn it into a raging fire. Personally, I know that my own flame has at many points been nothing more than embers, barely glowing. I know that I have given up on God a million times in my life, but He has never once given up on me. He keeps me here in this world, giving me more time and more chances.

We live in a valley and death casts its shadow over us all. We can be swallowed by it any time. We are only here today because God, through supernatural effort, has kept us here. He holds death back with His hand. One day, when we have reached our conclusion, for better or worse, he will let go and let it take us. From there we will enter eternal life or eternal damnation based not on what we have done or achieved, but on where we were already going.

If we were following the Evil One down into the depths, that is where we will land. But if we were following Christ up the mountain, we will ascend after death to its peak. And here's the really beautiful and remarkable thing: it doesn't matter how far we've climbed. All that matters is that we have begun. Christ does not say "get to this point here," or "you must make it over that first peak." He says only, *Come. Start your journey now. It doesn't matter where you've been. It doesn't matter what you've done. It doesn't matter who you were before. Repent of those ways, leave them down there in the dark, in the shadows, and come with Me. There is joy and glory at the top. But you must come now. There is no time to waste.*

A man may live his life in the shadows and be saved in the end because he took just one step up. A man may take many steps up the mountain but be destroyed in the end because he gave up too soon and started to descend back into the valley. A man may climb up, and lose his grip, and trip at certain points, and hurt his shoulder, break his leg, knock out a tooth, and still find the top at the end because he kept going in spite of it all. The main thing is just to climb.

I once lived an empty, secular, materialistic life. I am a Christian today not because of any virtue of my own, but simply because I got tired of living in the dark and feeling the cold. I had seen all that was ugly and selfish within myself, and I did not want to look upon it anymore. I opened the door to God because I felt that I had no choice. I had searched for happiness in the world and I had never found it.

I had eaten at its banquet and I was still starving. The world was too empty, my hunger was too severe, the knocking was too loud. I opened the door because what else was I supposed to do? It was not an act of courage. It was an act of desperation. And I felt for a long time that my embrace of the Christian life was cheap and false precisely because it was so desperate. But now I understand that desperation is exactly what God wants from us.

We all must take our first steps towards God on our knees, whimpering and pleading with Him. *Lord, I am desperate,* we must cry. *I hate my sin. I hate my loneliness. I cannot go on like this anymore.* Our prayer need not be specific. We do not need to tell God our long-term goals. We do not need to make any dramatic promises. We do not need to present a five-year plan. We must simply come to God, into His presence, and fall at His feet in total exhaustion. We must crawl to Him in our brokenness, in our sin, in our despair, in our confusion, in our desperation, and surrender. It really is as simple as that.

What Do You Want?

In *The Great Divorce,* C. S. Lewis describes an afterlife where any soul can enter paradise if only that soul really wants to. "No soul that seriously and constantly desires joy will ever miss it," he says. But the problem is that the damned souls do not actually desire joy.[3] The joy God offers—the only kind of joy available anywhere to anyone—is a joy of selflessness, adoration, and love. Many will decline the offer because they do not want to let go of their petty lusts, pride, hatred, or whatever other stupid little thing they have organized their life around.

We get what we want. That is the beautiful and terrifying truth. The final interrogation on Judgment Day will not be very extensive. We will not be quizzed about how much we gave to charity, or how many old ladies we helped across the street, or how many hours we spent praying. Those things are all good and important in their way, but they are not the point. When our time comes and we are standing before the throne of judgment, God, I imagine, will only need to ask one question, and it is the simplest and most fraught question anyone can ever ask: *What do you want?* And we, for the first time, will be forced to answer honestly, as we stand there in that place where no lies can be uttered.

I fear that a great many of us complacent Christians will have no choice but to look back at Him, knowing that we are seeing Him for the first and last time in our pitifully wasted lives, and say, "Myself, Lord. I want myself. Only myself."

Yet I pray, and I have hope, that you and I will be able to answer, with gratitude and joy, "You, Lord. You are what I have been searching for. You are the answer to every question I have asked. You are my reason and my purpose. You are my hunger, my longing, the aching in my bones. I have lived my life in pursuit of you, Lord. And now I just want to come home. Please, Lord, let me come home."

No matter which answer we give to that fateful question, I am sure that God's response will be the same: "So be it, my child. As you wish." Then two doors will open before us—one to life and one to death. And we will simply walk through the one that we have chosen.

Notes

Chapter One: Christians Not Worth Killing

1. The Holy Bible, New International Version (Zondervan, 2011). Unless otherwise noted, all scripture citations are from the New International Version (NIV).
2. "Age of First Exposure to Pornography Shapes Men's Attitudes toward Women," American Psychological Association, August 3, 2017, https://www.apa.org/news/press/releases/2017/08/pornography-exposure.
3. Mary Margaret Olohan, "California Implements Extreme New Sex Ed Curriculum," The Daily Signal, July 9, 2019, https://www.dailysignal.com/2019/07/09/california-implements-extreme-new-sex-ed-curriculum/.
4. "U.S. Abortion Statistics: Facts and Figures Relating to the Frequency of Abortion in the United States," Abort73.com, https://abort73.com/abortion_facts/us_abortion_statistics/.
5. "Global Christianity—A Report on the Size and Distribution of the World's Christian Population," Pew Research Center, December 19, 2011, https://www.pewforum.org/2011/12/19/global-christianity-exec/.
6. Marty Haugen, "All Are Welcome," GIA Publications, 1994, https://hymnary.org/text/let_us_build_a_house_where_love_can_dwe.

7. Jeremy Weber, "Christian, What Do You Believe? Probably a Heresy about Jesus, Says Survey, *Christianity Today*, October 16, 2018, https://www.christianitytoday.com/news/2018/october/what-do-christians-believe-ligonier-state-theology-heresy.html.

Chapter Two: The Broad Road That Leads to Destruction

1. "Religious Landscape Study," Pew Research Center, https://www.pewforum.org/religious-landscape-study/.
2. Cristina Maza, "Christian Persecution and Genocide Is Worse Now Than 'Any Time in History,' Report Says," *Newsweek*, January 4, 2018, https://www.newsweek.com/christian-persecution-genocide-worse-ever-770462.
3. The Associated Press, "Pope Francis Says Coptic Christians Killed in Egypt Bus Attack Were 'Martyrs,'" NBC News, May 28, 2017, https://www.nbcnews.com/storyline/isis-terror/pope-francis-says-coptic-christians-killed-egypt-bus-attack-were-n765561.
4. Justin Wm. Moyer, "Starbucks 'Removed Christ from Their Cups Because They Hate Jesus,' Christian Says in Viral Facebook Video," *Washington Post*, November 9, 2015, https://www.washingtonpost.com/news/morning-mix/wp/2015/11/09/starbucks-removed-christmas-from-their-cups-because-they-hate-jesus-christian-says-in-viral-facebook-video/.

Chapter Three: Just Believe

1. Dietrich Bonhoeffer, *The Cost of Discipleship* (London: SCM Press, 1959), 45.
2. The Holy Bible, King James Version.
3. John Henry Newman, *Parochial and Plain Sermons* (San Francisco: Ignatius Press, 1997), 535.
4. Bonhoeffer, *The Cost of Discipleship*, 89.

5. Graham Greene, *The Power and the Glory* (New York: Penguin, 2015), 211.

6. Kathy Johnson, "(Catholic) Scott Hahn vs. (Protestant) Bowman Salvation Debate #2 of 3," YouTube, June 12, 2017, https://www.youtube.com/watch?v=DEa7Try-V2Q.

7. C. S. Lewis, *The Great Divorce* (New York: HarperOne, 2015), 25ff.

Chapter Four: My Buddy Jesus

1. Christina L. Myers, "Baptist Church Removing Jesus Statue It Deems Too 'Catholic,'" Fox News, May 30, 2018, https://www.foxnews.com/us/baptist-church-removing-jesus-statue-it-deems-too-catholic.

2. Notanumber, "Dr Robert Jeffress: Be Grateful You Haven't Been Shot in the Head," YouTube, September 25, 2017, https://www.youtube.com/watch?v=KiAe_qvmBo8.

3. Henry Chadwick, trans., *Saint Augustine: Confessions: A New Translation by Henry Chadwick* (Oxford University Press, 1991), 201.

4. Depeche Mode, "Depeche Mode–Personal Jesus (Official Video)," YouTube, October 26, 2009, https://www.youtube.com/watch?v=u1xrNaTO1bI.

5. Charles Taylor, *A Secular Age* (Belknap, 2007), 40.

Chapter Five: The Gospel of Positivity

1. Christomlinmusic, "Chris Tomlin–Nobody Loves Me Like You (Official Music Video)," YouTube, October 11, 2018, https://www.youtube.com/watch?v=SG_IXFEO8yE.

2. Tim Challies, "The False Teachers: Creflo Dollar," @Challies (blog), May 29, 2014, https://www.challies.com/articles/the-false-teachers-creflo-dollar/.

3. Joel Osteen, *Your Best Life Now: 7 Steps to Living at Your Full Potential* (New York: Hachette Book Group, 2004), 1, 6.

4. Osteen, *Your Best Life*, 228–29.

5. Cath Martin, "Victoria Osteen Responds to Critics: 'I Did Not Mean to Imply That We Don't Worship God,'" Christian Today, September 6, 2014, https://www.christiantoday.com/article/victoria-osteen-responds-to-critics-i-did-not-mean-to-imply-that-we-dont-worship-god/40353.htm.

6. Fyodor Dostoevsky, *The Brothers Karamazov*, trans. Constance Garnett (Random House, 1996), 72.

7. "Listen to the Cry. . . ." Soren Kierkegaard Quotes, Brainy Quote, https://www.brainyquote.com/quotes/soren_kierkegaard_152204.

8. C. S. Lewis, *Till We Have Faces: A Myth Retold* (New York: HarperCollins, 1984), 86–87.

9. LongforTruth1, "Joyce Meyer Is Not a Sinner," YouTube, July 17, 2014, https://www.youtube.com/watch?v=NhDBwJVQv_0.

Chapter Six: Diabolical Vanishing Act

1. C. S. Lewis, *The Screwtape Letters* (HarperSanFrancisco, 2001), ix.

2. "Most American Christians Do Not Believe That Satan or the Holy Spirit Exist," Barna, April 13, 2009, https://www.barna.com/research/most-american-christians-do-not-believe-that-satan-or-the-holy-spirit-exist/.

3. Jonathan Merritt, "Barbara Brown Taylor on the Devil, Death, and the Definition of 'Christian,'" Religion News Service, April 15, 2014, https://religionnews.com/2014/04/15/barbara-brown-taylor-hell-death-means-christian/.

4. Paul A. Lance III, "Jesus Is Tempted/Tested by the Devil," First Congregational United Church of Christ, February 11, 2018, https://www.uccalpena.org/single-post/2018/02/11/Jesus-is-TestedTempted-by-the-Devil.

5. Gavin Ortlund, "Did Augustine Read Genesis 1 Literally?" Sapientia, Carl F.H. Henry Center for Theological Understanding, September 4, 2017, https://henrycenter.tiu.edu/2017/09/did-augustine-read-genesis-1-literally/.

6. The Holy Bible, King James Version.

7. Fyodor Dostoevsky, *The Brothers Karamazov*, trans. Constance Garnett (Random House, 1996), 118.

8. William Lane Craig, "Doctrine of Creation (Part 26)," Reasonable Faith with William Lane Craig, April 3, 2013, https://www.reasonablefaith.org/podcasts/defenders-podcast-series-2/s2-doctrine-of-creation/doctrine-of-creation-part-26/.

9. *Report I of the 40th Statewide Investigating Grand Jury*, Office of Attorney General, Commonwealth of Pennsylvania, July 27, 2018, https://www.attorneygeneral.gov/report/.

10. Trent Horn, "Is the Road to Hell Paved with the Skulls of Priests?" Catholic Answers, September 5, 2018, https://www.catholic.com/magazine/online-edition/is-the-road-to-hell-paved-with-the-skulls-of-priests.

11. "California Couple Plead Guilty to Torturing Their 13 Children," Reuters, February 22, 2109, https://www.reuters.com/article/us-california-captives/california-couple-plead-guilty-to-torturing-their-13-children-idUSKCN1QB28C.

12. Daniella Silva, "Georgia Dad Justin Ross Harris Sentenced to Life in Son's Hot Car Death," NBC News, December 5, 2016, https://www.nbcnews.com/storyline/hot-cars-and-kids/georgia-dad-justin-ross-harris-sentenced-life-son-s-hot-n692086.

13. Noah Hurowitz, "Texas Mom Gets 40 Years in Prison for Trying to Sell Her Toddler Daughter for Sex," Oxygen, July 17, 2018, https://www.oxygen.com/crime-time/sarah-marie-peters-texas-mom-gets-40-years-prison-trying-sell-toddler-daughter-sex.

14. Joan Carroll Cruz, *Angels & Devils* (TAN Books, 1999), 168.

Chapter Seven: Strength in Numbers

1. Bob Dylan, "The Times They Are A-Changin'," Bob Dylan, http://www.bobdylan.com/songs/times-they-are-changin/.

2. C. S. Lewis, *Surprised by Joy: The Shape of My Early Life* (HarperOne, 2017), 252.

3. Pius X, "Pascendi Dominici Gregis: Encyclical of Pope Pius X on the Doctrines of the Modernists," Vatican, 1907, http://w2.vatican.va/content/pius-x/en/encyclicals/documents/hf_p-x_enc_19070908_pascendi-dominici-gregis.html.

4. Billy Hallowell, "Oprah Asked This Ex-Megachurch Pastor When Christianity Will Embrace Gay Relationships—and His Answer Seemed to Take Her by Surprise," The Blaze, February 17, 2015, https://www.theblaze.com/news/2015/02/17/oprah-asked-this-ex-megachurch-pastor-when-christianity-will-embrace-gay-relationships-and-his-answer-seemed-to-take-her-by-surprise.

5. Jonathan Merritt, "The Politics of Jen Hatmaker: Trump, Black Lives Matter, Gay Marriage and More," Religion News Service, October 25, 2016, https://religionnews.com/2016/10/25/the-politics-of-jen-hatmaker-trump-black-lives-matter-gay-marriage-and-more/.

6. Lisa Bourne, "Fr. James Martin Rebuked after Urging Catholics to Support LGBT Pride," LifeSite News, June 4, 2018, https://www.lifesitenews.com/news/father-james-martin-catholics-shouldnt-be-conflicted-about-gay-pride-month.

7. See, for example, Steven Ertelt, "Christian Pastors Bless Late-Term Abortion Clinic and Its Staff, 'All They Do Is for God's Glory,'" Life News, February 1, 2018, https://www.lifenews.com/2018/02/01/christian-pastors-bless-late-term-abortion-clinic-and-its-staff-all-they-do-is-for-gods-glory/.

8. A. W. Geiger, "5 Facts on How Americans View the Bible and Other Religious Texts," Pew Research Center, April 14, 2017, https://www.pewresearch.org/fact-tank/2017/04/14/5-facts-on-how-americans-view-the-bible-and-other-religious-texts/.

9. "Views about Abortion," Pew Research Center, http://www.pewforum.org/religious-landscape-study/views-about-abortion/.

10. "Views about Same-Sex Marriage," Pew Research Center, http://www.pewforum.org/religious-landscape-study/views-about-same-sex-marriage/.

11. Inés San Martín, "Pope Francis Changes Teaching on Death Penalty, It's 'Inadmissible,'" *Crux*, August 2, 2018, https://cruxnow.com/ vatican/2018/08/02/pope-francis-changes-teaching-on-death-penalty-its-inadmissible/.

12. Saul McLeod, "Solomon Asch—Conformity Experiment," Simply Psychology, December 28, 2018, https://www.simplypsychology.org/ asch-conformity.html.

13. Anna Brown, "Republicans, Democrats Have Starkly Different Views on Transgender Issues," Pew Research Center, November 8, 2017, https:// www.pewresearch.org/fact-tank/2017/11/08/transgender-issues-divide-republicans-and-democrats/.

14. Gregory A. Smith, "Views of Transgender Issues Divide along Religious Lines," Pew Research Center, November 27, 2017, https://www. pewresearch.org/fact-tank/2017/11/27/views-of-transgender-issues-divide-along-religious-lines/.

Chapter Eight: The False Virtues

1. Marty Haugen, "All Are Welcome," GIA Publications, 1994, https:// hymnary.org/text/let_us_build_a_house_where_love_can_dwe.

2. C. S. Lewis, *The Great Divorce* (HarperOne, 2015), 25ff.

3. Joe Mita, "This Is Water by David Foster Wallace Full Speech," YouTube, May 5, 2013, https://www.youtube.com/watch?v=PhhC_N6Bm_s.

Chapter Nine: In and of the World

1. Emily Yahr, "'Scandal' Stuns Viewers with Abortion Scene in the Season's Winter Finale," *Washington Post*, November 20, 2015, https://www. washingtonpost.com/news/arts-and-entertainment/wp/2015/11/20/ scandal-stuns-viewers-with-abortion-scene-in-the-seasons-winter-finale/.

2. Carey Lodge, "Family Guy Airs Controversial Jesus Episode, 'The 2,000-Year-Old Virgin,'" *Christian Today*, December 8, 2014, https:// www.christiantoday.com/article/family-guy-airs-controversial-jesus-episode-the-2000-year-old-virgin/44070.htm.

3. Nick Allen, "Catholic League Complains After Larry David 'Urinates' on Jesus Painting in 'Curb Your Enthusiasm' Episode," *The Telegraph*, October 29, 2009, https://www.telegraph.co.uk/news/religion/6463624/Catholic-League-complains-after-Larry-David-urinates-on-Jesus-painting-in-Curb-your-Enthusiasm-episode.html.
4. Rod Dreher, *The Benedict Option: A Strategy for Christians in a Post-Christian Nation* (Sentinel, 2017).
5. The Holy Bible, King James Version.
6. "CCD Quick Facts," Common Core of Data: America's Public Schools, https://nces.ed.gov/ccd/quickfacts.asp.
7. Anthony Esolen, *Out of the Ashes: Rebuilding American Culture* (Washington, D.C.: Regnery Publishing, 2017).

Chapter Ten: Disorganized Religion

1. Jefferson Bethke, "Why I Hate Religion, But Love Jesus: Spoken Word," YouTube, January 10, 2012, https://www.youtube.com/watch?v=1IAhDGYlpqY.
2. *Merriam-Webster*, s.v. "organize (v.)," https://www.merriam-webster.com/dictionary/organize; *Merriam-Webster*, s.v. "religion (n.)," https://www.merriam-webster.com/dictionary/religion.
3. C. S. Lewis, *Mere Christianity* (HarperCollins, 1980), 46.
4. Urban II, "Speech at Council of Clermont, 1095, according to Fulcher of Chartres," [from Bongars, *Gesta Dei per Francos*, 1, 382 f., trans in Oliver J. Thatcher, and Edgar Holmes McNeal, eds., *A Source Book for Medieval History* (New York: Scribners, 1905), 513–17], Internet Medieval Sourcebook, Fordham University, https://sourcebooks.fordham.edu/source/urban2-fulcher.asp.

Chapter Twelve: Heaven for Everyone

1. Joel Osteen, *Your Best Life Now* (Hachette Book Group, 2004).

2. John Henry Newman, *Parochial and Plain Sermons* (Ignatius Press, 1997), 8.

3. C. S. Lewis, *The Great Divorce* (HarperOne, 2015), 75.

Index

Chesterton, G. K., 86

Christian entertainment industry, 59, 61–62

Christian pop music, 59–60

Civil War, 15

compassion, 112, 120–25

Confessions, (Saint Augustine), 52–53

Craig, William Lane, 86

Creation (of the world), 81

cross
as sufferings that Christians must bear, 8–9, 18, 21, 28, 32, 38, 51, 77, 123, 177
Christ's, 9, 17, 34, 38, 42, 44, 57, 61, 76–77, 85–87, 107, 157, 172

cross-dressing, 2–3

Crucifixion, 37, 57

Curb Your Enthusiasm (television show), 131

D

dark night of the soul, 35

Dawkins, Richard, 64

Devil, the. *See* Satan

divorce, 2, 9, 97–98, 112, 116, 131

Docetism, 96

doctrine of cheap grace, 28

Dolan, Timothy, Cardinal, 129–30

Dollar, Creflo, 66–68

Dostoevsky, Fyodor, 65, 72, 84, 173

Dreher, Rod, 136

Duck Dynasty (television show), 64–65

Dylan, Bob, 95

E

Easter, 37, 59

Egyptian martyrs, 16–17

Elijah (prophet), 31

End of Faith, The (Harris), 72

Esolen, Anthony, 138

Eve (in the Bible), 80

Ezekiel (prophet), 81

F

Facebook, 19, 55, 58, 124, 133, 149, 181

Fall, the, 80

Family Guy (television show), 131

First Crusade, 155

forgiveness, 9, 159, 163–65, 167

Francis (pope), 45, 98

G

Garden of Eden, 80

gay marriage, 96–99

gay pride, 97

gender fluidity, 103, 139

gender spectrum, 103, 139

Gethsemane, 15

Gnostics, 147

God's Not Dead (movie), 61–65

Good Christian Bitches (television show), 131

Gospel of Positivity, 57–77

grace, 20, 28, 30–31, 40, 42, 49, 71, 122, 161, 163, 165

Great Divorce, The (Lewis), 40, 183

Greene, Graham, 39

H

Hahn, Scott, 40

Harris, Sam, 72

Hatmaker, Jen, 97, 101

hatred, 25, 125–28, 175–76, 183

Hawking, Stephen, 65

Heaven, 8–9, 25, 30, 32, 39–41, 113, 118, 121, 123–24, 157, 163, 166–67, 172–73, 177–81

Hell, 8–9, 14, 20, 25, 31, 40, 57, 76, 81, 83, 88, 92–94, 121–22, 131, 160, 162, 172, 181

Hitchens, Christopher, 64

Hollywood, 21, 69, 103, 131–32, 143

Holy Spirit, 9, 17, 84, 176

homosexuality, 2, 98–101, 114

I

Impastor (television show), 131

Incarnation, 37, 96

indifference, 22, 125, 176

Inquisition, 62

Instagram, 58

internet, 20, 54, 106, 116, 132–34

Isaiah, 47–48

Islam, 16–18, 50, 115, 149

Israel, 89

"It Is Well with My Soul" (Spafford), 60–61

J

Jake, T. D., 67

James, Saint, 29, 44, 66

Jeffress, Robert, 51

Jehovah's Witnesses, 96

Jeremiah (prophet), 89, 174

John Chrysostom, Saint, 88

John of the Cross, Saint, 35

joy, 17, 33, 57, 70, 77, 90, 112, 117–18, 160, 166, 169, 172–73, 175, 177, 179–84

Judgment Day, 107, 115, 183

judgment, 4, 8, 81, 118–20, 184

K

Kierkegaard, Søren, 73, 171

L

Lance, Paul, 80

Last Supper, 150

Bible Verses